Maureen's Story

A 32 year love affair with Highclere Castle

By Maureen Cummins

Cover design and typesetting by:
Mouse House Print Shop, The Barn, Bath Place, Hale, Cheshire, WA14 2XY   (0161 929 5538)

Typeset on Apple Macintosh

Mahogany
c/o Mailblazers, 12 Appleby Glade Industrial Estate, Swadlincote, Derbyshire DE11 9EU   (01285 552 592)

Printed and bound by Ashford Colour Press Ltd, Gosport, Hampshire   (01329 229 700)

ISBN: 0-9552004-0-7

ACKNOWLEDGEMENTS

DAVID CARRICK
He took a chance on me writing a book. Thanks to him my story has been told.

LINDSEY GILES
Your patience, understanding and friendship were great treasures to me.

TONY HOGAN
Surprises are not a thing I can deal with, but my grateful thanks to you for all your efforts.

IAN CARNABY
Thank you for being such a treasure and the binding element that made this book possible.

ZELDA LAWRENCE-CURRAN
If you don't like the order of the chapters then she's to blame. But her help was invaluable.

There are two people who would have enjoyed my book and had a few laughs over it, but sadly they both died. My thoughts are with you Bill Porritt and "Queenie" Gold.

 Contents

Foreward

This is a hauntingly poignant and often hilarious 32-year love affair and a privileged portrayal of some of the people who lived and laughed within the walls of Highclere Castle.

It isn't a diary – it would have been an easier book to write if it were. Rather, it's a retrospective. I walked into Highclere Castle as a naïve assistant cook and left 32 years later a House Manager and I am rightfully proud that this wonderful house was entrusted to my care. I didn't own it, though some days (if I'm honest, most days) I thought I did, but its welfare belonged to me and I belonged to it.

I'd like to say that my days at Highclere were the happiest days of my life. This book is especially for my son Chris. He'd be justified in wishing that I'd loved him a little more and Highclere a little less, but there we are.

In addition I also dedicate this book to Adrian Wiley who, like me, loves Highclere Castle as though it were his own and without whose dedication and hard work Highclere would not have found its rightful place on the map.

Maureen Elizabeth Cummins

How it all began

It's strange to think that I ended up in one of the grandest stately homes in England when my own beginnings were so humble. I was one of six, born into a working class family in Seaham, Co. Durham. My father worked most of his life as a coal miner except during the war when he was in the RAF. We all moved to Stoke-on-Trent during the mid Fifties as prospects in the mining industry were more promising there. The four eldest in the family were known as the four M's – Michael, Margaret, Maureen and Malcolm, who was my twin. Mum then lost a child and David, the youngest, was born 10 years later.

My desire to earn money started at an early age and everyone in Seaham must have breathed a sigh of relief when I departed at the age of five for the Potteries. Apparently I earned money by collecting empty milk and lemonade bottles from doorsteps to get the deposits back and I would then put the money in my savings. I cleaned shoes at sixpence a time (which is 2½p in today's money). Later, during my time at Pinewood School and Meir Secondary Modern, I always had some scams going to earn a few bob. I passed my exams for catering college in Stoke-on-Trent but, to my dismay, I wasn't allowed to go as my parents couldn't afford it.

I didn't know life would be so hard at 11. I cleaned my teacher's house twice a week in the evenings and then, as I grew up, Friday evenings and Saturdays were spent stacking shelves at the local Co-op store. Later on I worked on a fruit stall at Longton market.

I was anxious to earn money to get away from home. As with many families in the fifties and sixties money was tight and rows about it were constant. I thought if I left home it would lighten the burden. Another reason was that my eldest brother was constantly interfering with me in bed. My dad caught him once and from then on a lock was put on the door. I couldn't talk to anyone about this, even though I knew that it was wrong and it put me off men for a long time. After my parents died I found out that he was actually my half brother.

I couldn't understand why no one seemed to care for me. My mother didn't love me then and never did throughout her life, and made no bones about it after my father died. That may have been why I became so independent with a desire to explore and tackle the world. I suppose I was determined to show her what I was made of. I had a fierce individualistic streak allied to a certain bluntness which stayed with me all my working life.

To explain why I'm writing this book I have to go back to when I left home at 15. I was a normal teenager, full of dreams and ambition and determined to make something of myself. All my brothers and sisters were in the Army or Navy but when I went to join the Army they wouldn't accept me, mainly because of my weight and height. I was very persistent and tried three times but received the same answer. I felt I had so much to give but no one wanted me.

First I got a job with Beswick's in Longton but after a week I knew I couldn't be somewhere where I wasn't happy in my work. This led to my finding a live-in job at the Metropole Commercial Hotel in Stoke-on-Trent as a general assistant. I cycled 4 miles there and back for the interview. Mrs Pasterla, who ran the hotel with her husband (they were Italians), put me through my paces in a variety of departments. I stayed there for $3\frac{1}{2}$ years and gave everything to the job. My mum and dad were mortified that I went ahead and did all this without talking to them about living away from home.

Every Friday Mrs Pasterla would check for dust in the bedrooms. She used to put ten-shilling notes, half-crowns or sixpences under carpets and on top of wardrobes to see if you were honest and cleaned efficiently. I got a bit fed up with it after a few weeks as I didn't want anyone to feel I was dishonest so I turned round and said to her that if I found any more money I'd keep it.

Another way I found I could earn money was by pressing newspapers and reselling them after guests at breakfast had read them – you couldn't do that now, of course. I lived in and worked split shifts. Dad came to check on me once a week.

I then did a seasonal job at the Lakeside Hotel in the Lake District for six months. When I went for the interview the manager rang Mr Pasterla for a reference and said he'd given me a poor one. I was 'very hot-headed, arrogant and definitely not a good worker', apparently. When I got over the shock I told the manager I'd work for a month for nothing if that turned out to be right but, if I proved Mr Pasterla wrong, I should be given a job. He took me on as general assistant for my cheek, I showed what I could do and stayed for the summer.

My head was full of fantasies. I wanted to do something and be somewhere special, making my dreams come true. I knew I wasn't brainy but I was practical and the experience I'd gained through various jobs, hotels, and prep school would stand me in good stead. My season at the Lakeside Hotel in Cumbria was coming to an end and I had to think seriously about getting another job. I knew I wanted to cook, but I was also looking for something a bit more challenging and unusual. Since leaving home, The Lady magazine had always helped me find work and I travelled overnight on the coach to London from Cumbria after seeing an advertisement in the magazine which read: 'Good right hand needed, apply box no, etc'. Which was definitely me.

I caught a train from London to Newbury, a bus to Highclere Village and walked to the Castle via Highclere Church. I arrived for the interview on 20th August, 1968. Eventually I was stopped in the park by Jack Day, the electrician.

"Hello Missy. Where are you going?" he said.

I told him that I had an interview with Ivy Rogers, the cook, for a job in the kitchens. I jumped into his mini and he took me to the Castle. As we approached the front drive I knew instantly that I had made the right decision. The Lake District was beautiful but Highclere was magnificent. There was a mystical look to the place – arrogance and beauty within a magnificent building. My feelings brought on great excitement and I was convinced the job as assistant to the cook was mine even before the interview.

Mr Day took me to the back entrance and rang the bell. The butler came to the door – his name was Mr Taylor. Ivy Rogers, the cook, followed him. Oh my, what had I done? It reminded me of Upstairs Downstairs, the programme about life in Victorian times. Ivy was very friendly and took me into the staff room (now part of the tea rooms) at Highclere Castle. Apparently she thought I was very suitable and we went into the kitchen. And what a kitchen it was! In the middle was a great wooden table with brass containers down the centre, large wooden chopping boards either side and clean towels looped over the side rails. At the end there was a beautiful marble slab for pastry. There was a large cast-iron range run by coal with a slow oven above. To the right was a baking oven for scones and bread. Lots of cupboard space. Above the range they hung the hams. There was a pestle and mortar, the biggest I'd ever seen. Near the pastry room there was a cupboard full of Minton china with a huge tavern clock on the left of the range. On the wooden shelves there were copper saucepans and lids. There was a huge walk-in fridge and a very large pastry room. It really was a Victorian style kitchen. The vegetable room had deep wooden sinks where Ivy's daily, Kate Crocker, prepared all the vegetables.

Ivy couldn't understand why I hadn't discussed the job with my parents. I was so determined to take it that I agreed to tell them and, if they approved, I could start work on 1st September, 1968. At the end of the season the manager of the Lakeside Hotel asked me to stay on as a member of staff for the winter. Unfortunately I had to decline as I'd already been to Highclere. The Lakeside Hotel has lots of wonderful memories for me and my education began there. But my world had started to expand and I wanted to expand, too. I was determined to keep pursuing my dreams. I convinced my parents that I'd settle down and that was how I arrived at Highclere and stayed for 32 years.

Now I can relay to you my love for Highclere, the people I met, the film stars and royalty. I can talk about the Herbert family, the trials and tribulations of my work and how it affected my home life. You will see that I was sometimes arrogant and had a very singular view of the people affecting my world. I shall try to show how they changed my outlook on life and made me see things in a different way. You will also see how my love for Highclere nearly cost me my job as I clung to my old-fashioned ways, ideas and the conviction that I was always right.

My first impressions of life at Highclere

1st September 1968 was my first day as the 6th Earl of Carnarvon's assistant cook. You could say that I had very high expectations. I had a half-day off each week and my wage was £3 per week with split shifts. Wednesday until 6pm was my half-day. I had to return by 6pm in order to prepare the evening meal for Lord Carnarvon and the staff although later I was allowed a full day when I went to Newbury College to do a City & Guilds course in domestic cookery. I passed with distinction.

When I first had the idea of earning a few extra bob I never thought it would come from washing the 6th Earl's cars. Bill Misson, the chauffeur, used to hate the job. An American Cadillac was my first job, and I started on half a crown (12½p) per car. It was an automatic and very easy to drive. I also used to clean the old Land Rover that the estate kept for shoots. I got three old shillings for this as it was always so dirty. As time went on I earned extra money by working for Pat Withers, the painter and decorator. I also cleaned the house and walked the dogs at Highclere Kennels a few afternoons a week. I also had a talent for cutting hair and gradually built up a small clientele on the estate. I had about 12 customers in the end and they would come and see me in my spare time.

I bought a motor scooter from the estate, paying them a few shillings a week out of my wages, as the nearest bus was two miles away. I was able to travel a little now and had my independence.

People were very conservative in the south and I felt they needed cheering up. I didn't mean to be cheeky or forward, it was just that everyone up north seemed to be that way. Mind you, I could never understand why people up there spent most of their lives in smoky pubs or working men's clubs. I do now, though – it was their way of relaxing after a hard day's work. My parents were Methodists and didn't approve, so that's why I felt it was wrong and never joined in. They were trying to give us the right sort of upbringing, I suppose, without realising they were shutting me off from the outside world.

During those early days in the kitchen one or two interesting little things occurred. For example, Kate Crocker, the daily, wouldn't eat or taste salmon. Ivy couldn't understand it but then it turned out that Kate had only tasted tinned salmon and hated it. Eventually we persuaded her to try fresh salmon and she loved it from that moment on. There were times when my friend Pat and I would have to go to the local pub to get the beer for the ham as the 6th Earl loved boiled ham in draught beer, but we had to take the ham and container with us. It was huge. Another thing that fascinated me was seeing the bombe mould of ice cream filled with tutti frutti, then covered with meringue and put in the oven to brown (baked Alaska). I'd never seen anything like it in my life.

I had to skin and paunch rabbits and hares. I could handle this if they were cold but I was always in an awful mess when the hares were done as the blood went everywhere instead of in the bowl. The 6th Earl always gave Captain Forsyth-Forrest, the stud manager, jugged hare when he came for lunch as he'd once said he liked it, but he was only being polite and actually hated it. Ivy and I used to laugh because the 6th Earl used to ask the head keeper to get the hares especially for the Captain.

We used to put everything through very large sieves in those early days because liquidisers didn't exist. All sorbets and ice cream were made and turned by hand in a container bucket; then rock salt and ice were put around the container and the connecting handle was turned by hand for two hours. Cooking was generally done in the copper saucepans. To whip eggs or whites everything was done by hand in copper bowls over hot water. What a godsend it was when later we had a Kenwood mixer and liquidiser – heaven!

We had a wonderful marble slab which kept pastry so cool we made excellent puff pastries. Whenever we had fish on the menu the 6th Earl always told his guests that Ivy, his cook, had risen early and gone to collect it from the Hamble River. He didn't realise we had all our fish freshly delivered from Mac Fisheries in Newbury!

We pickled freshly laid eggs from our own chickens into crock-pots ready for the winter months. And there were pickled walnuts from our own walnut trees, which are still there. We made quince and japonica jellies, homemade jams and marmalades and bottled all our own fruits, peaches, nectarines, plums, damsons and much more besides as we had our own orchards. The peaches, pears and nectarines were grown in the top gardens, as they are today, and were all bottled, poached or frozen ready for winter and the shoots. Throughout the seasons everything was fresh and utilised accordingly.

My room, called 'Dormer', was on the top floor of the Castle and the housemaids lived on that floor as well. Ivy lived on the estate near the cricket pitch. Robert Taylor, the butler, lived in Butler's Cottage in the park; his widow, Joan, still lives in the same house. Bill Misson, the chauffeur, his wife Julie and their two children lived in a house in the courtyard. Jack Day, the electrician, lived with his wife and daughter in Day's Cottage near the kitchen. Francis Reid, the very strict Austrian housekeeper, and Jock Reid the head gardener lived in a little bungalow that was converted from the old pump house behind the workshops. Jock died on the front lawn a few years after I arrived. He had always produced new potatoes in pots in March ready for the 6th Earl's return from the Bahamas. Alfie, a part-time odd job man, worked as a postman in

Newbury, and there was also Charlie Crocker, the local Highclere postman who cycled across from the village. Mrs Furness became postwoman when Charlie retired.

The Estate Office was originally located in a wooden prefabricated building near White Oak House but later moved into the courtyard and is still there. Miss Stubbings was the estate manager and Albert Saxton, who lived in Clere Lodge, was her assistant. Mary Povey was Lord Carnarvon's secretary and Mr Soper was the clerk of works. Ernie Haines was the plumber, like his father before him. Tommie Butcher was the solicitor for the Castle. Pat Hayes (now Pat Withers) and her father were the painters and decorators on the estate. Charlie Maber was the head keeper. The kitchen gardens were tended by Derek Cramme, John Crocker and two under-gardeners. They all lived in estate houses nearby.

Despite all these people living in or around the Castle, in those early days I was very lonely at Highclere. I wasn't a good mixer and consequently had very few friends. On one occasion I wasn't feeling very well and my imagination starting running wild. What if something happened to me? Would anyone care? On this particular evening, just to get attention from someone, I feigned a collapse on the bathroom floor. Alice the chambermaid came upstairs and found me and called Mrs Reid. A doctor was called and, to my amazement, wanted me rushed into hospital overnight. What I'd forgotten was that earlier in the day I'd slipped and fallen, banging my head on the floor. I later found out that I actually had concussion. Needless to say I never tried anything like that again because it scared me silly.

My LP's were a godsend and two in particular that I used to play all the time were *Ebb Tide* and *The Righteous Brothers Greatest Hits*. Thinking that no one could hear the music as there weren't any staff around I used to open the windows of my room and play the records to my heart's content. Until, that is, I was nearly throttled by Shirley Greene, a lady who worked for Mrs Reid and lived in Castle Lodge. She met me one day and said: "If you ever play that bloody music again I will personally murder you". Baffled, I hadn't realised the sound travelled the distance to the lodge. I certainly kept my head down after that and my windows remained closed.

I'd worked with a girl called Alice – though she preferred Annice – at the Metropole in Stoke-on-Trent. She came over from Ireland to work here, like a good many others. She was quite a bit more experienced than I was but nevertheless wrote to ask if there was any work in the house. I knew the housekeeper needed someone, so I recommended her and she got the position. I'd worked with her for two years previously but when she came to Highclere her character changed. She became very toffee nosed with ideas well above her station, in my opinion. She was always broke because money was needed back home in Ireland, so I helped her out many times. She didn't stay long as she was summoned back home. Unaware of the situation in Ireland, and being a totally trusting sort of person, I gave her the fare on the understanding that she would return the money. Now I know what a chump I was. She wrote a few letters to keep in touch, but her last one astounded me. Her brother and father were members of the IRA and it was best not to write again as they didn't want her being tempted back to England. I never did see my money.

14

Personalities and life at Highclere

ROBERT TAYLOR – 1ST FOOTMAN AND BUTLER TO THE 6TH EARL

Robert Taylor became 1st Footman to the 6th Earl of Carnarvon in 1936. Robert travelled with the 6th Earl many times to America as butler/valet, on one occasion visiting the State Rooms of the White House, Washington DC. He even went on Concorde.

When Robert came to Highclere there were 16 staff:

4 in the kitchen (1 cook + 3)
6 house staff (1 housekeeper and 5 housemaids)
5 in the pantry
1 butler

When I arrived in 1968 the staff consisted of:

Robert   –   Butler
Alfie   –   Odd job person
Mrs Reid   –   Housekeeper
Ivy   –   Cook
Kate   –   Daily
Jock Reid   –   Head Gardener
2 Assistant Gardeners
2 Dailies part-time

Sometimes we'd have relief butlers and later we had Jenny Oakley (later Hughes when she married the head-keeper) to help. But that was still only ten people to run the gardens and house – which was very different from the day

Robert arrived in 1936. Robert had great affection for Jenny because she was the daughter he never had. When I first came to Highclere I was like a little dumpling anyway and Jenny was like a blonde bombshell, slim and trim.

In my presence Robert told Lady Carnarvon that she was the Lady of the House and that she was the one to give me my orders, not he. This did not go down well with Lady Carnarvon as Robert was almost shouting at her. Lady Carnarvon was very embarrassed and I think she might have killed him on the spot, but to her credit she never said a word. I really felt for her. She took everything in her stride and I have the greatest respect for her.

Robert held Highclere together for many years, even after the 6th Earl died and the 7th Earl took over and the first caterers, Sarah Corbett and Mary Brown of Sarah & Mary Catering arrived. He helped the 7th Earl with the inventory for probate and was involved in the discovery of the Egyptian artefacts which will be discussed later in this book.

During the two years of being open to the public it was Robert who taught me how to look after the silver, wind the clocks and lay a table professionally. I had many things to be grateful for but it took me quite a while to appreciate how much Robert's way of life had affected me. For instance, he gave me my taste for vintage wines, introduced me to the wine cellars and taught me how to decant properly.

Robert Taylor died on the 23rd July, 1990 after lunch at home. On the day he died, chaos reigned because he'd locked all the cellars and had the keys and we were hosting an evening reception for Hampshire County Council. Everyone thought it wouldn't go ahead but we struggled through somehow and from then on a duplicate set of keys was always kept in the alarm cupboard. Robert's 54 years at Highclere were a great achievement. He saw changes pre-war and post-war. He was a perfect butler in every way, a great professional and his loyalty to Highclere was never in doubt.

MISS CRYSTAL STUBBINGS – ESTATE MANAGER TO THE 6TH EARL

When I arrived at Highclere in 1968 Miss Stubbings was the estate manager for the 6th Earl of Carnarvon. Robert always remarked that, when she arrived after the war, it was on her bicycle with all her possessions in two carrier bags hanging from the handlebars. I always thought this was an amusing story. She was a very clever woman who took her job personally and seriously. Out on to the estate she'd go to find out what was needed and talk to the workers. I wasn't too involved with her during this period, although she did occasionally come to lunch or dinner at the Castle. The estate offices at that time were based near White Oak House, close to the sawmill on the estate.

As the years progressed she often had her young niece, Hilary, to the Field House where she lived and both were invited to the Castle. Hilary was a very naughty child and I always dreaded it when she came to the Castle. The 6th Earl's comments about her were always very rude when he came down to the kitchen the next day. It was often rumoured that the 6th Earl was Hilary's father because initially they came to the Castle so often, but I know it wasn't true. Hilary's father was killed abroad suddenly so Miss Stubbings took her under her wing as she was family, after all. The 6th Earl wouldn't have sired anyone so naughty. Later he avoided asking her because sometimes she was uncontrollable. Hilary improved slightly as she grew older and eventually married and had two sons. Her sons were like a whirlwind when she came to visit me at Stable Cottage.

I got to know Miss Stubbings better when she asked me to be her housekeeper on a part-time basis following my abrupt dismissal from the 6th Earl's service; more about that later. I became aware of her strength of character one day when she went to a coffee morning for Save the Children, a charity Lady Carnarvon supported, at Milford Lake House. She walked through the park, past the sawmill and took the scenic route to Milford Lake. A part of the bridge she was crossing gave way and she hurt her leg quite badly. After a few months it hadn't healed so Miss Stubbings took the 7th Earl to court to claim compensation for having an unsafe bridge with no notice attached. The 7th Earl was hopping mad. The best, however, was yet to come. The 6th Earl had given the Field House to Miss Stubbings for her services, loyalty and companionship. She lived in it for a while and then sold it back to the 7th Earl, as she wanted to be closer to her sister in Kings Lynn. She certainly had the last laugh on the 7th Earl and remained at Weasingham St Peter until her death, leaving the property to Hilary and her family.

She was a wonderful person to me, but Stan Anstie, who worked on the estate, always jumped whenever he saw her. On her day off in midweek she'd stay in bed and take only water and fruit, claiming it cleansed the system and was good for the soul.

MARY POVEY – SECRETARY TO THE 6th EARL

Mary Povey arrived in February 1968, the same year that I came to Highclere. She was the 6th Earl's secretary and had a good rapport with him. At this time Miss Stubbings had an office opposite the 6th Earl's study, so I saw a lot of both of them. The 6th Earl gave Mary a horse called Honey and eventually gave her Sammy the donkey to keep, as well. Lady Carolyn, the 6th Earl's granddaughter, saw Sammy when he was a foal at Newbury's annual show. He – the 6th Earl – had the foal weaned and cut and then bought it for Lady Carolyn. When she outgrew Sammy it was decided the donkey should be given to Mary as company for Honey. Mary and Albert Saxton, estate manager after Crystal Stubbings' retirement, shared the vet's bill and food.

Mary continued to work in the office when it moved from White Oak Lodge near the cricket pitch to the stable courtyard in the Georgian part of the Castle. When she retired, Lindsey took over the reins and became secretary to Lord Porchester and Albert Saxton. To me, Albert was always the "rock" at Highclere, steadfast, reliable and a mentor to Geordie, now the 8th Earl.

MRS FRANCIS REID – HOUSEKEEPER TO THE 6th EARL

Mrs Reid, the housekeeper when I first came to Highclere, was Austrian and came to England during the Second World War. Housekeepers, like people in all other jobs, come in different categories. Often housekeepers were spinsters. They had their own sitting room and quarters and no one was allowed to enter. They were always called Mrs as a mark of respect. Down through the ages they oversaw the housemaids and the still room maids (the women who made the preserves and the cakes). They looked after the household linen and were responsible for the staff quarters. Normally butlers, housekeepers and cooks would work closely together. Many housekeepers would stay with a family for 30 to 40 years, always keeping a close eye on the female quarters. Before any male visitor could visit he had to pass the housekeeper and get permission. Mrs Reid was originally a housemaid at a house in Woolton Hill and married Jock Reid, who was the head gardener at Highclere. She always looked after the ladies when they arrived for parties at the weekend, unpacking for them, laying out their evening clothes, washing any underclothes where necessary and turning down the beds in the evening. Sometimes ladies would bring their maids to attend to their needs. A housekeeper or a ladies' maid would call their guests or lady in the morning with a casual "good morning", draw back the curtains, then put the tea tray beside the bed. They would also be expected to pack their suitcases on departure. Most guests, if they had been properly looked after, would tip the housekeeper or maid for all their services. If ladies didn't come down to breakfast it was the housekeeper's or ladies maid's duty to take the breakfast tray up to them.

I did not actually get to know Mrs Reid until we sat down one evening in the staff room (now the tea rooms), to watch the very first episode of Emmerdale Farm. Jock had died by this time and Mrs Reid, like me, was on her own. Our friendship grew slowly, as work commitments did not give us the time to get to know each other. During the four weeks when the 6th Earl was away in the Bahamas, we would get together twice weekly to watch Emmerdale and enjoy a glass of wine. It was during one of our evenings together that I discovered that Francis (she spelt her name with an 'i') had been blessed with a son who, sadly, had died when he was just 10 years old.

I used to love listening to all her stories about Austria and the people she knew, especially the old man who lived in the mountains and made his own cheeses, living off the land. She also told me about the mountain sun gleaming on the horizon and the harshness of nature that everyone had to bear. Even the old man used to come down from the mountain just before the winter snows to live in the village. Francis would tell of the differences between the snow in Austria and the snow in England and how, when she was young, people would have to dig themselves out before they could go to work or the children get to school.

Francis was a fascinating person. She had a great love for gardening, very strong coffee and a dedication to Highclere and the 6th Earl which I had not encountered before. After she retired (when the Castle opened to the public), she developed diabetes and, later, cancer. My friend Jenny and I looked after her through her remaining days and Hildegard, an Austrian friend, would come occasionally from the Isle of Wight to visit her. Lady Carnarvon (the 7th Earl's wife) and Francis were firm friends throughout her lifetime at Highclere

When Francis died she left Jenny and myself £1,000 each and, unexpectedly, the remainder of her estate to Hildegard. This turned out to more than £25,000 and, as one of the executors, I was amazed because she always seemed to be penny pinching – not buying coal that she needed and doing various other things that pensioners do to hold on to their money. It turned out that a long time before, Miss Stubbings had invested some money for Francis and I am sure she did not realise the value of her estate. Money could not replace the loss of such a friend and she gave me my first opportunity to go abroad – to Austria, of course! The country was everything that Francis had promised and I loved it. When she died, she was actually the first person I had seen in a coffin. She was at peace, a waxed formation, finally with the ones she loved and about to meet again her beloved family and her precious cat Polly, whom she adored.

BILL MISSON – VALET AND CHAUFFEUR TO THE 6Th EARL

Bill Misson hailed from Ireland and was originally the 6th Earl's valet and chauffeur. However, by 1986, when Robert Taylor had semi-retired and the 6th Earl was not in the best of health, Misson had taken over some of Robert's duties. At this time the 6th Earl's meals were mostly pureed and he used the boudoir as a bedroom, having meals on a tray either in his room or in his study.

Even though Misson fought with the 6th Earl he was very fond of him. Head gamekeeper Eddie Hughes reminded me recently of the time when Bill, having taken over following Robert's death, served the 6th Earl dinner at 8pm sharp. "Tonight, my Lord, you shall have dinner in the dining room as a special treat, instead of having it on a tray in your study", he announced. He even dressed up in one of the three jackets he'd bought (actually paid for by the 6th Earl) and wore the mauve one to serve dinner. Unfortunately, when I arrived with the food, there was Misson in his mauve jacket but His Lordship had turned up in his pyjamas. To crown it all, when dessert was served (compote of raspberries), Misson poured the cream straight from the carton instead of using a silver jug! He was a character, all right.

At this time the Castle was closed and shuttered most of the time and guests had stopped coming. Misson quite often asked if I'd come over and trim his Lordship's hair and cut his nails, which I was happy to do.

My early years at Highclere during the 6th Earl's life

As I say, when I arrived at Highclere it was all Upstairs, Downstairs – a step back into the Victorian era. The 6th Earl of Carnarvon was a jolly Earl and he loved entertaining, shooting and racing parties, and playing bridge with the ladies afterwards. He was a very warm, loving kind of person. Mr Harry (the 7th Earl's second son) used to tell the tale –   which no one actually believed, though I'm quite sure it was true – of how his grandpa used to hide in the wardrobe in 'Mercia' (one of the bedrooms) and jump out on the ladies when they started undressing for bed. That's why there was never a key to Mercia until we opened to the public.

Robert always came across as the person in charge because he was the butler. He used to lock me out in the evenings when I had an evening off or when Lord Carnarvon was away. I didn't fear him and I wouldn't say he had a grudge against me exactly, but there was this attitude of: 'I'm in charge and that's it'. Of course, I was very defiant and full of myself. I enjoyed the challenge of getting into the Castle when Robert was out, so I devised different ways. There were three different methods, and I could still manage at least one of them today.

I used to go up the fire ladder, across the roof and through the door at the top of the servants' stairs that I'd left unlocked when I went out. Of course, the fire ladders have been reduced now that we're open to the public. I was a lot more agile in those days and I knew the roof like the back of my hand. He could never figure out how I used to get in. He stumped me one evening, though. I actually got in through the pastry room window and he'd bolted all the doors in the kitchen, so I had to sleep on the living room sofa, which was my sitting room. The following morning at about a quarter to seven Malcolm Clarke, the window cleaner, came in to get some water. Malcolm (who now has his own office cleaning business) still relates how shocked he was to find me in the kitchen, but he never let on to Robert and is still a friend of mine today. I actually managed to get up to my room, have a quick shower, change and come down and start Lord Carnarvon's breakfast. That baffled Robert and he continued to have it in for me until our relationship mellowed.

Jack Day used the entrance near the boiler room and this was another way in, once I found out how to get the 8" heavy metal key off the chain. Try to imagine carrying this key around with you! But at least it gave me another option and it was closer to the servants' stairs; the alarms were not connected to that area then with the staff living in. I didn't think I was clever, it was just a bit of mischief and enabled me to put one over on Robert.

There were times when I got back into the Castle and flashed the torch three times to let my friend Pat know that I'd made it. She used to wait along the top road until I was in safely. Pat was the one who taught me how to ride my motor scooter. As usual, I listened attentively as she explained how to use the gears and brake. But, in my eagerness, I was actually going through the motions as she spoke. Off I shot towards the mill near the cricket pitch! Blimey, she hadn't told me how to stop and there was a huge hedge coming up. Luckily for me Pat was in hot pursuit on her Garelli bike, shouting like mad and telling me how to stop.

All I could do was laugh; I was as mad as a hatter and would do anything for a good time. I used to stop at Pat's on my day off sometimes and hated her Westminster clock which chimed every 15 minutes. Under one of its feet it had two matchsticks to keep it in time. These came out when I slept on the couch and were put back before I left. It was a long time before Pat found out and didn't she give me hell – it was a family heirloom.

We went everywhere on our bikes, drank many glasses of homemade wine, went bowling in Southampton and enjoyed evenings at the Red House, our local. Robert found out that I was staying at Pat's and I was totally banned from staying out overnight. Was I livid! I stopped out even later and still managed to get the better of him on many occasions. Who did he think he was, anyway? That was my attitude in those days.

I remember the time we had a big party for Mr Harry's birthday and Lady Carolyn's coming of age at Highclere and Robert was so strict he wouldn't even let us go and see The Queen when she entered the front door. It was only through Mrs Reid, the housekeeper, who allowed us to peer through the stone balustrades on the landing, that I was able to see Her Majesty. We had music outside with Joe Loss and his orchestra and everyone went through the music room window via a wooden staircase. As they were going up over the steps the 6th Earl used to feel the ladies' bottoms.

We had our ups and downs at Highclere but we also had our little bits of fun, especially as Robert was very strict with all the staff. We had Filipino and Irish girls, and he tried to keep us on a tight rein like all butlers of that era. We weren't allowed to go through the House without his permission; we always used to use the servants' stairs.

The only time I was actually allowed through the main part of the House was when Ivy went on holiday and I had to do the menus with Lord Carnarvon, quite often when he was having his bath. He used to say, 'Come my dear, sit your fanny down here and I'll have a bath'. In America your fanny was your bottom, but it sounded rather funny hearing it for the first time here. Misson (the valet) didn't seem to have a problem with it and I think I was so naïve then that I just accepted everything. Michael van der Woude, the 6th Earl's nephew, was very fond of Jenny because she was so attractive. He used to hide behind the pillars on the saloon landing waiting for her to pass, then jump out naked in front of her when she was going about her evening duties. The 6th Earl also used to wander around the landing naked, so we were all fairly used to seeing them without any clothes on and that's why it never bothered me when I did the menus while the 6th Earl was in the bath. It was only when Robert stepped in, because he wanted to protect Jenny, that Michael was not asked back to Highclere so often.

The 6th Earl was a very genuine and generous man in his time. He gave the world his memories in the form of two books – *No Regrets* and *Ermine Tales*. Mrs Betty Brown typed all the copy for both books. He excelled himself when asked to be a guest on Parkinson on BBC TV. He was so magical that he was asked back to talk about his second book. He wrote wonderful comments on the flyleaf of my parents' copies of the books.

I went down to help Robert and Mrs Reid in the drawing room on one occasion and couldn't understand where all the furniture had gone. Later I found out that Lord Carnarvon had sold it. All that remained in the room were tin baths with champagne bottles in and trestle tables. It was then that I saw the little cupboards between the two doorways and Mrs Reid said: 'Don't let Robert catch you looking in there'. I didn't realize then that these were the Egyptian Artefacts – though many of the staff at that time knew of their existence. What's more, Bill Misson's children used to play with them when Robert wasn't around.

We used to have a tavern clock in the kitchen and I kept it dead on time by the radio. I was only allowed a radio in the kitchen when Ivy wasn't there and I always checked it, but Robert said it was completely the wrong time and we had to go by his watch. We had many arguments over that. Later I used to keep the clock 15 minutes fast to give me time in case things did go wrong and to allow for any other eventuality. Robert cottoned on to this and had a word with Ivy, but she agreed that it was a good idea to keep the clock fast and in fact it got us out of a few sticky situations during 16½ years in the kitchen.

Working with Mrs Reid was fascinating and something of a revelation. We became particularly good friends when she semi-retired. There were many interesting things which came to light, including a rug beater, a long handled brush with extensions looking like a Turk's head which was used, apparently, to brush the stonework to get rid of cobwebs, the only problem being that you needed muscles like Mike Tyson's in order to use it.

The equipment Mrs Reid used in her time differed considerably from the equipment I employed in my day. She would use the Turk's head brush for cobwebs etc, whereas I would use an extended lambs' wool fluffy or, for areas out of reach, a helium-filled balloon tied with pure wool and extended to the height of the ceiling. You then pulled the wool up and down and bounced it off the ceiling or stonework (I needed about 10 balloons), and it was a very effective way of cleaning out of the way corners. To clean carpets Mrs Reid used a hand sweeper whereas I used a cylinder and upright vacuum cleaners. Stone bottles and copper warming pans were used to air and warm the beds in Mrs Reid's day, but I used hot water bottles and electric blankets. For lighting, candles were employed by Mrs Reid whereas torches and lamps were used in my era.

There were still slipper-shaped bedpans, chamber pots, glass inhalers and throat sprays in some of the cupboards. A hip bath and a tin bath were still stored in the cellars. Although these baths were put to their original use in their own time, when I was at Highclere they became excellent containers for ice to chill bottles of champagne and wine. Chamber candlesticks were still in use when I arrived in 1968 but they were stored away when the Castle was opened to the public.

Linen hand towels were replaced by terry towels and bars of soap gave way to liquid soap in dispensers which became the "in" thing. Machines with scrubber heads were used as an alternative to scrubbing floors by hand. A floor brush and liquid polish with a buffer machine became popular, owing to the shortage of staff, and gave you a rest from hard polishing the floors on your hands and knees. Some things were a welcome bonus. Brass wadding replaced liquid Brasso and was less messy when used to clean brass.

Amongst other recollections from the past are the cone-shaped cylinder fire hydrants and buckets of sand and water. The water buckets had a hand pump next to them for spraying the water. These once useful features were dotted around the Castle. In their time they were the latest in fire safety, but modern observers would find them falling a long way short of the required standard. Indeed, when we opened to the public the fire officer had a field day, as you can imagine. When I arrived, fire drills consisted of jumping through a canvas chute on the top floor of the Castle and speeding down to safety on the ground. Mr Day the electrician conducted all the fire drills – no doubt by candlelight.

The Castle

As you know, I fell in love with Highclere Castle at first sight. When I arrived in 1968 we weren't allowed to roam around at will in case the 6th Earl or Robert Taylor caught us. I was very envious of the people who worked upstairs in the house as I worked only in the kitchen and, whilst I was down there, I saw practically no one. As I lived in the Castle we had to approach our rooms via the servants' staircase near the dining room. Halfway up the stairs there was a fire door and, when I could (Robert having gone home after lunch for a few hours), I would sneak around the house exploring some of the rooms. Peering into the rooms gave me quite a surprise. I hadn't realised that the house I was working in had such magnificent, extravagant furnishings. I surmised that the Earl must be a very rich man, but that didn't deter me. I was really excited about it all. I was totally bowled over. It was really posh; I wasn't used to such grand surroundings.

Oddly enough the Castle WAS a castle, but it had no battlements like a normal one. It was, in fact, a Victorian manor house designed to look like a castle to show off the wealth of the 3rd Earl of Carnarvon. He even had his motto carved everywhere around the house. It read UNG IE SERVIRAY, Latin for 'One only will I serve'. Later I felt this didn't apply to me as I'd worked for three Earls (including the 8th Earl when he was still Lord Porchester). Apparently, the 3rd Earl wanted a very grand home to impress all his friends so he commissioned Sir Charles Barry, the architect responsible for the Houses of Parliament, to design it. The 4th Earl continued his father's work and engaged Thomas Allom to complete the interiors.

Highclere was such a magnificent place. The front hall had what were to me a very funny-looking pair of dragons protecting the entrance hall. Later I found out that they were called Wyverns, the heraldic beast of the Carnarvon family. They came in many forms, such as fire dogs (metal supports for logs in a fireplace) or carvings and were scattered all around the house.

There was a Library next to the entry hall and it looked so cosy with its dark mahogany painted columns, gilded bookcases and rich red curtains. The Library was split into two sections, the main library and the 'small' library, which was easily spacious enough to contain a very large concert grand piano near the window. Behind the piano was a red curtain, and, curiosity getting the better of me, I had to take look behind it. It was actually one of the corner turrets of the house which was filled with junk at the time, though there were signs that at some point it had been used as an office. The main Library was huge, the furniture and carpets really expensive and luxurious. It was a world of treasures and a fantastic place to explore. There was a famous desk, made by George Bullock, and a chair in the library which had belonged to Napoleon Bonaparte.

I was in total awe, but I knew it wasn't all going to be a bed of roses where work was concerned. Ashes from the fire needed emptying and that proved a difficult task because the huge fireguard took two people to lift. The fireplace had to be black leaded in order to maintain its black gloss effect, and this was all double-dutch to me. The carpets throughout the house had to be hoovered with an old cylinder hoover. It appeared that the life of a housemaid wasn't just about meeting famous people and basking in glory, it was a very hard job with many different aspects to it and only the housekeeper and butler would come into contact with the guests in any meaningful way. It was their responsibility to meet and greet them and look after their needs, such as unpacking their clothes and preparing their things for the next day.

On one occasion when a housemaid was showing me the library I was looking at the bookcases when I glanced out of the window and saw something quite beautiful. A building across the huge lawns sat in splendour. It was a folly, one of many on the estate, and was called Jackdaw's Castle. Its purpose, like that of all follies, was to attract attention. The other follies on the estate (Heaven's

Gate, the Temple and the Grotto) were also strategically placed to attract the eye. I was so engrossed that I didn't notice the housemaid had disappeared. I was a little worried because, after all, I was not supposed to be up in the main house. I called out softly to see where she was and she replied from behind a bookcase: "Come through the books". I was amazed to find that what I thought was another bookcase was actually a hidden door, covered with false bookends. I would never have guessed it. Opening the door brought me to the music room with its hand-painted ceiling in the baroque style, Italian embroidery, gilt panels and fabulous red curtains. The room had no carpets, only oak floors which had to be polished to a high shine. Apparently this was a hands and knees job. Most of the polishing was done by Mrs Hawes who was one of the housekeeper's daily helpers, the other being Mrs Bradd. I thought at the time how funny it was to have a music room but still have the piano in the library; folk were strange.

Next we went into the drawing room. Well, this was such a light and beautiful room and the wallpaper was fantastic: it wasn't until later that I discovered it wasn't actually wallpaper but silk! And there were silk curtains to match – can you imagine how much it all cost?! Central to the room hung a glorious chandelier; the sunlight was streaming through the window making it glitter and sparkle. The ceiling in the room was gilded on top of moulded mounts of plaster, but it was in a bit of a state. With all this apparent wealth, surely they could afford to have the ceiling repaired? There were chunks missing all over, it was a heart-breaking sight.

There were paintings of the family from generations ago displayed on the walls. The next room I ventured into was the smoking room, which seemed to me a very dark and crowded place. The room featured a huge leather settee and chairs, some very fine furniture and lots of paintings. One in particular caught my eye: it was the central piece hanging over the fireplace and featured a dead swan and other game birds. It actually suited the sombre ambience of the room.

I skipped the next room, a ladies' boudoir, because it held no interest for me whatsoever. The adjacent room was the 6th Earl's study, so I didn't dare go in there for fear of being caught snooping around. If Robert had caught me there would have been hell to pay.

The heart of the house was called the saloon, which was massive and decorated, I later found out, in the gothic style. The walls were covered in leather, depicting hunting scenes. I never imagined that someone would cover walls in leather; these followed the silk coverings I had already seen, and I was amazed. I found out later that the leather came from Spain and was very old, even compared to everything else in the house. The room was furnished with a massive oak table in the centre which held two silver lamp stands and a floral arrangement, and there were two tapestry chairs, one on either side of the table. These were very old, apparently dating back to Georgian times. A huge pale pink settee and chairs accompanied by a Georgian stool occupied the near side of the room. All in all it was overwhelming. Under the main staircase there was a huge log cupboard, filled to the brim with logs. I was certainly glad I didn't have to keep it filled.

I found it all so unbelievable. How could anyone create such beauty? The fact that this was actually a home was amazing, too: my mind drifted back to times gone by when I imagined ladies in fine flowing gowns, escorted by their gentlemen friends or husbands, being greeted by the butler while a footman held open the door to the saloon, allowing them access to the heart of this beautiful home. A roaring fire would greet the guests and the hum of voices around the balustrades would give the place a glowing ambience, full of joy and laughter. This fantastic Victorian home was where I wanted to be, but just then the clock struck 4pm, startling me out of my reverie and back to reality. I realised that Robert would be back at any moment. On my way back downstairs I stopped to admire the tapestries that surrounded some of the walls on the staircase, which had to be oak. Great paintings hung on the walls, the subjects looking so stern and miserable but also very rich.

The next room was the dining room, which contained what seemed to me a very small table for such a huge house, with the walls covered in yet more paintings. These were of members of the family, apparently. The fireplace was surrounded by carvings of such beauty that, had I not seen it with my own eyes, I should never have thought it possible. The Library had carvings but these were something else, quite exquisite. (Little did I know that in years to come I would be polishing them.)

A quick exit back down to the kitchens was required when I heard footsteps coming from further back in the house. I quickly descended the concrete stairs that led back to the lower levels. This was my first real experience of the Castle and it was exhilarating, to say the least. Over the following years, I learned a great deal more about this magnificent Victorian home.

The magnificent front doors of the Castle became a challenge to me because they were always dark and dingy and not at all as they were supposed to be. It took hours of painstaking hard work to scrub off years of grime and linseed. Underneath was the most beautiful walnut wood, which was cleaned and polished to display the splendour of the grain. The doors remain in this condition today.

Contentment reigned as I gave my love to the Castle. I made more discoveries, such as the dining table which extended with twelve leaves to accommodate 26 people for dinner, thus transforming the small table I had seen in my earlier years to a huge, 27-foot long banqueting table. This was surrounded by leather-seated mahogany chairs, some of which were Chippendale and others Hepplewaite. They had to be stained and polished when worn to return them to their former pristine condition. The house was filled with paintings by Sir William Beechey, Sir Joshua Reynolds, Dutch artists, paintings in the style of Canaletto, and even a few by the great master Van Dyke; the list goes on.

The furniture and carvings were of more interest to me. I loved them and later discovered that some had been created by Grinling Gibbons. The exquisite oak staircase that descended into the saloon took nearly a year to carve and install. When I became housekeeper in 1988, I lavished plenty of care and attention on them and the carvings were always cleaned and polished. Although Gibbons was known for his limewood foliage carvings, his signature was actually peapods. The peapods told a tale of their own because, if they were open, Gibbons had been paid for his work. But if they remained closed, he was still awaiting settlement. He was one of the greatest decorative woodcarvers and one of the best-known craftsmen. It was a joy to feel I was in some way connected to his life and to be in a position where I could appreciate the work of a master.

Antics of some of the staff

Mr Luck was the relief butler when we were busy with shoots or racing parties while the 6th Earl was alive. He was the opposite of Robert and liked a good laugh and a few jokes. One of his favourite jokes was to go behind Kate Crocker in the kitchens and drop a tray behind her. She nearly died of fright but he found it extremely funny. Every time he came he did the same thing, but she never learned.

The housemaids went out with the chauffeurs when they came for a shooting party and Mr Luck didn't mind this as he was always out for a bit of fun. After visiting the Carnarvon Arms and having a good evening they all had coffee upon their return. Next day Mr Luck went to take the chauffeurs an early cup of tea. Guess what? No cups! He found a load of jam jars and took the tea up to the chauffeurs, only to find the housemaids in bed with them! My goodness, this gave him such a shock he dropped the whole tray of tea and told Robert he'd had enough and was going home.

Alfie, the odd job man, always helped Robert and the kitchen staff. One of the funniest things I remember is Alfie cooking live lobsters, a job he always took on because we couldn't stand the screeching when they went into the boiling water. I came in one evening to start work and found him chasing the lobsters around the kitchen as they'd jumped out of the large pot. It was hilarious but eventually we caught them and he put them back in the pot. I have never eaten lobster since that day.

Jack Day was the electrician/handyman during my years at Highclere and a firm favourite of the 6th Earl. He was constantly setting the alarm system off in the servery before we had a hi-tech system installed. Even after he retired he still toured the Castle to see if anything needed doing, like changing bulbs or repairing carpets. Apparently he always liked to use the servery loo – Robert said it was to save his loo paper at home! This was always a good joke.

Jack would always pull out the big circuit breakers from the distribution board without turning off the electricity, even though he knew the circuits were being changed. Quite often it would throw him against the wall, but he didn't seem to worry; as he said, 'a little bit of spark does you good'. Whenever he went out in his Mini and gave me a lift he'd turn the engine off going down the hill. "Why do you do that, Mr. Day?" I asked. "Well, Missy, it's to save petrol!" he replied. 'We always did this in the war'.

Originally the main central heating system had been run on anthracite. Ashes were emptied out every day and taken down the long corridor to get rid of them. This made everything very dirty, hence the conversion to oil. However, Jack always tried to light it as he did in the old anthracite days using paper and wood after it had been out for the summer.

Jack was always rooting around in the big Grundon rubbish bin and we used to laugh when we saw the ladder propped up against the side. Anything he could get his hands on that he could sell, he'd bring out. It was amazing in his later years that he didn't fall – he'd prop the ladder on the outside of the bin and then haul it over the top, put it inside the bin and climb inside. He was not a poor man, in fact he was one of the richest men on the estate. This way was his way of life and he enjoyed it and this is why we all thought it so funny.

My time at and around Highclere

1973 – 1987

I married Tony Cummins on September 1st, 1973. I desperately wanted a son and my parents wouldn't hear of living 'in sin'. My mother and I had terrible rows about Tony, but I married him anyway. I'd supported myself from the age of 15½ and hadn't asked them for any help. I even paid for the wedding. My present from my parents was £50, although in 1973 that was a lot of money.

As Tony had been married before, even Robert commented that I was marrying second-hand goods. This set me against him and it was a long time before he and I became friends. I was so determined to stay at Highclere that I asked Ivy the cook to put in a good word for me with the 6th Earl, which is how I came to live at Stable Cottage. The Misson family had moved from Stable Cottage into the flat above the tea rooms to be closer to the 6th Earl.

After an earlier miscarriage in 1975 my son, Chris, arrived on St. Valentine's Day 1977. It was a difficult birth, mainly because I wouldn't give up work, and I didn't see him for a few days as he was in intensive care with breathing problems. After six weeks at home I was anxious to get back to work – I really missed the Castle and the company.

Tony strongly disagreed with this but I was very determined to go back for two days a week and eventually on a full-time basis. Chris came to work with me and was my saviour really, because everyone adored him and that made things easier.

Head keeper Eddie Hughes and his wife Jenny were great friends of mine. We had loads of fun during our time at Highclere – Sarah, their daughter, was born the June following Chris and brought up at Highclere too, so he and she grew up together. We actually made half the kitchen into a nursery section and my sitting room was where Chris used to try to sleep in the morning. The current tea rooms were the housekeeper's room and that was where Sarah slept. This was the year of The Queen's Silver Jubilee. Oddly enough, my son's second name is Philip and Sarah's second name is Elizabeth.

Chris spent a lot of time with the 6th Earl during his younger years, following him around with his wheelbarrow so that the 6th Earl could put his clippings somewhere. The Earl used to drive the gardeners mad and eventually Misson had to hide his secateurs. Mary Povey continued to buy secateurs, Misson duly hid them and this went on for a few years. Nor was the fun restricted to the Earl – Bill Misson would post chocolate biscuits through the letterbox on pieces of string for Chris and the pair of them would play on the tea room lawn with Chris' toy tractor. Also, Bill would stand at the top of the staircase and throw money over the lawn so that Chris could collect it. One of the foreign notes was worth nearly £20 when we took it to the bank.

MY REDUNDANCY

I used to work full time until four years after I was married in 1973, then in 1977 Chris was born, and after six weeks I went back to work part-time. In the latter years of his life the 6th Earl lived in the area now called the boudoir, which was his bedroom; the study, bathroom and toilet were as they are now. For a year the bathroom and toilet didn't have any locks on them because the 6th Earl was always locking himself in. Mrs Yarnold was the 6th Earl's dearest friend and at one time it was thought they'd marry.

Bill Misson knew that Ivy wanted to retire and that she intended to see the 6th Earl so that I could take her place. Bill admitted he'd persuaded the 6th Earl that Julie (his wife) was better suited to looking after him than I, so he convinced Mrs Yarnold and the 6th Earl that I had no cooking talents at all. Bill always wanted his wife to take over, which is how I came to be made redundant – what a loss to Highclere! Until Bill Misson died I never found out the truth. He used to come to Ivy's once a week when he lived at Penwood. There were a good many occasions when we went over the old times with Ivy.

My redundancy came as a deep shock to me. As I recall I was hanging out my washing on a Monday – I only worked on Tuesdays and Thursdays to give Ivy and Julie their days off. I went to see Ivy to find out the menu for Tuesday and found her in floods of tears. I took her to my sitting room and then we had the full story.

"Oh Mo, you've got the sack!"

"The sack?" I said. "What for?"

"Lord Carnarvon wants you out".

"But what for?" I repeated.

"You didn't cook the dinner properly last night".

"You've got to be kidding me Ivy, no one can sack me for not cooking the dinner properly".

"He can and he has", said Ivy. "Apparently you didn't cook the soup properly".

"You're kidding", I said. "I didn't cook the soup, Ivy, you did and he had it cold anyway so how could I have done something wrong?"

Ivy said: "I'm sorry Mo, it's not my fault, I've already been to Lord Carnarvon but he won't listen to me. He says you're sacked and he doesn't want to see you around the Castle again".

"Ivy, what about my house and family? You know I haven't done anything wrong, why won't he listen to you?" I asked.

"You see, Mo, Bill wants Julie to take over in the kitchen and this is his way of getting you out. I can't do anything to stop him, I'm sorry."

"He's going to regret this Ivy, he can't do this to me!"

"He has, Mo, and you can't do anything about it", said Ivy.

"Believe me this is not the end, I'm going to see Miss Stubbings. She'll sort it out", I said.

Miss Stubbings was the estate manager for the 6th Earl at the time. On my way to see her I called in to see Mary Povey and Albert Saxton in the office. I was in a daze because I couldn't believe what had happened to me. I must have sounded so confused, and they couldn't come to terms with it either. Apparently Mr Saxton rang Miss Stubbings and told her what had happened. She was angry. Lord Porchester had also been informed and wasn't amused at all. However, when Miss Stubbings eventually sorted everything out it was the 6th Earl who was at a loss. He had to give me a redundancy payment of three months, I could remain in my house on condition that I cleaned Mr Saxton's office and the stud office twice a week and I was offered a part-time job housekeeping with Miss Stubbings. I also took on cleaning jobs in the village. I had 8 jobs in a week but I knew that one day I'd be back at Highclere Castle again.

My life while I was outside Highclere had its moments too. As I mentioned, after my redundancy from the 6th Earl I decided to find more work. Even though I kept the house and cleaned the two offices, I also had other cleaning jobs. One involved looking after Fred Sherman, a retired worker from the estate. Each day I would go down to his house and cook for him and tidy up. He'd been in hospital and couldn't face the thought of going into a home for the elderly. His sister Bessy had recently died from tetanus, having been infected by some rat urine on a bean stick. Fred was a relative of Jack Day's but they didn't get on very well. He always looked on Eddie Hughes, the keeper, as a son and bequeathed many personal items to him on his death.

It was a cold day as I approached Fred's, we'd had a good fall of snow overnight and Chris, who was only 4½ at the time, was very excited at the thought of playing in the garden. I had picked him up from playschool and was on my way to Fred's to prepare lunch and tidy up. Little did I know what awaited me inside. Every day Chris would take Fred's newspaper up to him while I did my bits and pieces. For some reason, fortune smiled on me. Chris, without a care in the world, headed straight for the garden and was having the time of his life in the snow. It was unusual for Fred not to knock on the floor, so I went up to see him. I was met by a horrific sight because he was sitting on the bed, as stiff as a board, with his shotgun held to his temple and his brains splattered across the bedroom wall.

I was sick to my stomach and just stood there, unable to take it all in. But then a new me took over. I thought first of Chris, playing happily in the snow, and knew I had to get him away. I kept thinking: "Must ring Ivy, she'll take care of him, just get him away", so I phoned her straightaway. Then I picked up Chris and rang the police and Jack Day. I knew Fred kept money in the house so when the police arrived I told them where it was. Jack Day came down but was not allowed to touch anything. Doctor Keeble arrived and put things in order.

What I didn't realise was that my subconscious had taken over and I was on auto-pilot. It wasn't until after the event that I came to terms with what had happened. There was a post mortem in Whitchurch and the burial, of course. The executors wrote and asked if I would clean and tidy the house as they lived in Wales, so that was the last thing I did for Fred. What a terrible way to end your life. What he couldn't bear was the thought of spending his remaining years in an old people's home. I must say I sympathised with that.

I had this strange, uneasy feeling that I should have known something was wrong. Sometimes I was troubled by Fred's mood swings, which fluctuated between elation and utter despair. He took out his boredom on me, but I couldn't do anything about it, couldn't share the burden with anyone else. Many times I racked my brains for a solution but unfortunately I was too naïve to cope. I had too many things going on in my own muddled world to recognise the signs of someone contemplating suicide. I shall feel guilty for the rest of my life that I couldn't help him, couldn't guide him towards a peaceful old age. No one will ever know how I felt or what I went through.

When everything had been sorted out I went back to do the cleaning and washing so that the estate could let the property, but the memory of that day will always be with me. Well, that was another episode in my life and one I've never spoken about before, so maybe writing it all down has been good for me.

Life wasn't simple, believe me, but I battled on – at least I was still around at Highclere. Nothing could get any worse. Miss Stubbings told me that I shouldn't go to my solicitor or a tribunal to claim unfair dismissal because I'd be given notice to quit my house. I thought her assessment of the situation was fair, probably because I didn't know any better and wanted to stay at Highclere.

Nor was I only the casualty at this time. Shortly after my own experience, Dave Radwell (the head keeper) was made redundant on New Year's Eve, 1985. The first thing he knew of this was when he was asked by Lord Porchester to go to the stud office. Dave was asked: "Have you ever thought about returning to Buckinghamshire?" – a rather strange way of starting a conversation.

Dave replied, "No, we've no thoughts of returning. Why?" Lord Porchester's response completely dumbfounded him.

"Well, I'm going to have to make you redundant as I can't afford to keep a head keeper and four other keepers as well. You were the first in so you'll be the first to go".

This was certainly not the way things had been handled before. Many times in the past Dave and Lord Porchester had crossed swords because Dave didn't agree with his way of shooting and during this meeting at the stud Lord

Michael and Margaret

Maureen and Malcolm

Where it all began - the Lakeside Hotel, Windemere, 1969

Ivy Rogers (6th Earl's cook)
and Rastus

Maureen in 1969
with the infamous scooter

Menu du

Potage Bonne Femme

Blanchailles Frits

Percolin Rôti
Légumes

Mandarine Mousse
Pâtisserie
Café

6th Earl's menus showing
the mysterious 'Percolin'

Menu du

Potage Tomate Thoed

Homard en Aspic
Sce Mayonaise

Percolin Rôti
Légumes

Soufflé au citron
Cerisses
Pâtisserie
Café

Robert Taylor

6th Earl of Carnarvon

Earl of Carnarvon with unidentified lady

(left to right)
aria, Francis Reid, Maureen,
Jenny Hughes (nee Oakley)

Francis Reid

Jack Day

aureen's wedding

Jenny Oakley and Eddie Hughes 1972

(left to right)
Maureen, Francis Reid with
Chris, Jenny Hughes with
Sarah

Telephone Highclere 253204
(STD Code 0635)

HIGHCLERE CASTLE,
NEWBURY.
RG15 9RN

12th March, 1982

My dear Maureen,

I have learned this morning that Christopher has been very unwell recently. I
do hope he is recovering rapidly and enclose
a little gift which I feel he will appreciate

I reiterate that I enjoy your cooking
immensely, as, indeed, last night's per-
formance clearly demonstrated!

With every good wish.

Yours sincerely,

Carnarvon.

Letter from 6th Earl to Maureen

Porchester had been telling him how to run the shoot. Dave told Lord Porchester that he worked for his father, not him, and he was the one he'd take his orders from. Naturally, that did not go down well with Lord Porchester. Dave Radwell received his notice but what they didn't realise was that he was nowhere near 65, he was only 59 – an expensive oversight on the estate's part because it meant they had to pay him more redundancy money. Dave felt the real reason for the appalling decision to make him redundant was that he considered himself to be working for the 6th Earl, not Lord Porchester, so therefore he thought his orders on a shoot should come from the former. Dave never received anything from the 6th Earl's will, as the rest of the permanent staff did, when the 6th Earl died in September, 1987. If Dave hadn't told Lord Porchester to "fuck off and leave him to run things", he would probably have lasted the course. Eddie Hughes took over as head gamekeeper but Dave Radwell and his wife Maureen continued to live in a rented property on the estate for many years until Dave's death in August, 2005.

THE END OF ONE ERA AND NEW BEGINNINGS

Eventually the 6th Earl of Carnarvon went into the Edgecombe nursing home and slowly deteriorated, sadly dying on the 22nd September 1987. He was buried at Highclere on Tuesday 29th September. The 7th Earl (formerly Lord Porchester) had the funeral and burial arrangements organized even before his father was dead. Sotheby's were called in to do an inventory of the Castle and shortly afterwards the Egyptian artefacts were discovered, which will be discussed later.

Following the 6th Earl of Carnarvon's death the family made the decision to open to the public. Bill Misson, who was on holiday in Yorkshire at the time, was sent a letter terminating his employment. He was given three months' notice following many years of service. Misson and his wife Julie went to see the 7th Earl on their return from holiday because the situation was serious and they had two sons to think of. Well, there had always been rows between Misson and Lord Porchester (the 7th Earl) but this was quite something. Bill hated the 7th Earl, mainly because the latter couldn't talk to the 6th Earl in his later years. Bill's abuse wasn't always called for, but it was justified in some ways. "Will you fucking well stand still when I'm talking to you?" Misson said to the 7th Earl after he'd been to pay his respects to the 6th Earl. The argument went on from the back door to the car, with Misson banging the door after Lord Porchester had got in. The argument was so loud that Mary Povey came out of the office to see what was happening. Misson yelled at Mary, "You can fucking well go and tell Lord Carnarvon as you're so far up his arse!" Misson had rowed with the former Lord Porchester so often I'm sure this was why his employment was being terminated. However, to give him credit the 7th Earl pulled some strings with the council to enable Misson and his family to get a council house at Penwood and they moved in over Christmas, 1987.

The 7th Earl must have known that Misson had leukaemia because, while they were in America together, he'd had an operation – which the 6th Earl paid for. Also, he was attending hospital for treatment, which was a regular topic of discussion between Robert Taylor and Ivy, the cook. Later, Misson died of leukaemia after organizing his funeral plot and wake. He is buried in Highclere Cemetery.

Following Misson's death, Lady Carnarvon employed Julie for ten years. Julie still lives at Penwood with her son Andrew, but the other son Gregory has no communication with his family, even though he lives nearby in Newbury.

Soon after the 6th Earl was lowered into the ground and his son inherited the title, the will revealed that all was not as expected. The 7th Earl inherited the Castle and grounds; his eldest son (the new Lord Porchester) inherited two and a half thousand acres around the Castle and the 7th Earl inherited the rest of the estate that surrounded this. In time, Lord Porchester became well aware of how valuable his land and its houses were to become. Other bequests included The Hon Harry Herbert, the 7th Earl's second son, being left Forge Cottage while Lady Carolyn, his daughter, received Laundry Cottage. Both were on the estate.

As I said earlier, the decision was made to open the Castle to the public and Tim Howland joined as Castle manager to help Harry look after the Castle during the run-up period until such time as he and Chica (his wife) could take full responsibility. Harry had found that he needed help to manage the Castle, due to the pressures of running his horseracing business as well.

There was a great deal to be done by way of preparation. Tea rooms had to be created, loos built, a gift shop and an exhibition set up. A car parking area had to be established, together with a ticket office. Mrs Reid felt she couldn't cope with the transition from domestic service to public opening and decided to retire as she was well over 80. I was then informed that I would be taking over as the 7th Earl of Carnarvon's housekeeper – I wasn't even consulted! I found out that Lord Carnarvon had apparently had a meeting with Sarah and Mary from Sarah & Mary Catering (who were the caterers contracted for Lady Carolyn's wedding) and Mr Saxton in the dining room. Sarah and Mary wanted their housekeeper from Foley Lodge to fill the vacancy of housekeeper at the Castle following Mrs Reid's retirement while Foley Lodge was being refurbished. However, Lord Carnarvon replied with a definite 'no' – Maureen was his housekeeper. Mr Saxton had to come across and tell me my position had now changed.

As from May 1988 I became the 7th Earl's housekeeper on £125 per month, hours as required; this was a big step up from assistant cook at £3 per week plus meals and accommodation. How things had changed! A local lady, Jean Devonish, came to help me and introduced me to the feather duster, which came in handy in years to come – especially when I had Mr Harry doing some dusting for the television programme *High Stakes at Highclere*. The Queen was visiting and we were waiting for her housekeeper, but the film crew decided to film Mr Harry helping me dispose of cobwebs in the saloon. However, the footage did not make the programme.

My position as the 7th Earl's housekeeper started on the 16th May 1988, but it was a very different type of housekeeping compared to the 6th Earl's era. It was on a commercial basis and the principle was the same, but at Highclere there were no guests staying or residential staff in the Castle, only the caretakers. In fact, the 7th Earl of Carnarvon had two housekeepers: Mrs Betty Gale was his main housekeeper at Milford Lake House (where he and the Countess resided), while I looked after Highclere Castle. Milford Lake House was a home in every sense because the children were brought up there and Betty looked after their everyday needs. Highclere Castle was a home on a commercial basis only. However, the same standards had to be maintained. The most important qualities for running a house are punctuality, organisational ability and cleanliness; those same qualities have passed down through the ages and have always been my guiding light. Household management is about keeping to a routine and getting certain tasks done on a regular basis to keep things up to a certain standard. Writing up a schedule helps. How things look shows the love and care given to a household and comments from guests to their host on visits made the job worthwhile during my time at Highclere.

Lord and Lady Carnarvon worked tirelessly to change Highclere from the gloomy, shuttered place it had become into a Castle which looked more like someone's home. In his last few years, the 6th Earl had allowed things to deteriorate, needing a woman's touch to arrest the slide. The Castle had to be stripped of hard polish, with a liquid polish applied to comply with regulations concerning the public. Carpets and curtains had to be cleaned or replaced. The interior designer Pru Lane-Fox came in to give advice and set about creating the fabrics which would maintain certain standards where the Castle was concerned. Mr Alexander from Boki's florists in Newbury was employed to create a large centre arrangement in the saloon as Lady Carnarvon liked fresh flowers. The gardeners had to provide pot plants everywhere. The boudoir had to be refurbished because in later years it had become the 6th Earl's bedroom. Ropes and posts had to be made and carpet runners purchased to protect existing carpets. Sotheby's came to advise about paintings and relocated furniture to the appropriate rooms. The paintings were cleaned and the gold leaf restored.

Stan Bosley (who worked at the time for Stewart and Turner Antique Dealers) came to advise and restore those antiques needing more attention. Stan had restored a walnut pedestal desk for the 7th Earl when he was Lord Porchester. When the 6th Earl died, the 7th Earl asked Stan to come and give his opinion on repairs needed to the furniture to bring everything up to scratch with public opening imminent. Stan's first restoration was the fireplace in the smoking room where, over the years, soot, dirt and grime had accumulated over everything. Underneath, a beautiful pine fireplace was revealed. Stan was also responsible for restoring many of the antiques in the Castle over the 10 years that he worked there. The highlight of that period came when the 7th Earl introduced him to The Queen, who was visiting the Castle.

The Withers from Highclere were called in to decorate the boudoir and the 6th Earl's study. This involved specialised paintwork and decorative finishes but, even though their work was highly thought of, they were paid only the basic rate. The colours in the boudoir were chosen to complement Lady Carnarvon's grandmother's portrait which hangs there. During the touching-up of paintwork in the saloon, Mike Withers was asking for suggestions because no one had managed to get the correct colour of the ageing stonework. My suggestion of liquid coffee, a touch of paint, juice from some teabags and a little dirt and gravel soon did the trick and has stood the test of time. Just another handy hint!

It took two days to clean the oak shutters, sanding them down as they were all white where the sun had bleached them, with four coats of polish bringing them up to the required standard. And it took two days – and six flasks of tea – to clean the chandelier in the drawing room as it hadn't been attended to for several years.

I was now responsible for looking after the Castle and its contents, and many things had to be repaired and replaced in order to be ready for the opening. The furniture from the drawing room, which had been sold by the 6th Earl, was replaced with similar French-style pieces. Channel 4, who were making the programme *High Stakes at Highclere*, filmed the tattered curtains in the music room which were going to be replaced for the opening, but it was put back until the 1994/5 project. Cabinets were purchased so that the Egyptian artefacts could be displayed in the music room.

As the kitchens had to be refurbished it was very difficult to decide what to throw away. A large skip was ordered and the whole kitchen sorted out. Brasses and copper, though, were put upstairs for safekeeping. A few plates monogrammed with the entwined C's were kept (and copies were later sold in the gift shop). No one seemed to know what else should be retained. The kitchen table, which had originally been built within the main kitchen, had a chainsaw put through it for easier removal. Once again a reminder of a distant era had disappeared. Sarah & Mary moved in shortly afterwards to take over the catering, using the kitchens as a base for their outside work. The kitchens were upgraded to meet health and hygiene regulations. The housekeeper's room and staff room were made into the present tea rooms and an archway installed. They were then refurbished. It was also necessary to obtain a licence to sell drinks and, later, a separate licence to conduct civil ceremonies for weddings as initially the 7th Earl did not allow wedding receptions at the Castle.

The saloon carpet was repaired. Although very valuable, there were many holes and it was held together with tacks and tape. One hole had 136 tacks around it (this was discovered when the carpet was replaced for Geordie's – the new Lord Porchester's – wedding). The curtains in Queen Caroline bedroom were turned upside down and repaired and a new carpet bought. This was made into an exhibition room covering the history of the Castle.

As Highclere was now a commercial business and no longer a private house, fire precautions were essential. The only major fire systems worthy of mention were the main water system and the hoses. This system was incorporated on each floor and fed from a reservoir. Hoses were replaced and modern hydrants were installed, although some of the old systems were retained for historical, if not practical, value. Fire exits were put into operation and a plan for evacuation in case of fire was implemented, similar to the plan in operation at Windsor Castle.

Security was another issue. During the early days the 6th Earl was burgled twice. The gardens were opened for viewing once a year and, on one particular occasion, members of Burghclere Horticultural Society were visiting. The 6th Earl went to the office in the courtyard but left a window open. All of his small ivory elephants – and he had many, ranging from very tiny to very large on the mantelpiece – and crested wax letter seals were stolen. On another occasion thieves broke in through the window on the stairwell outside the boudoir. The long case clock in the saloon was taken, but had only been carried halfway across the lawn when Robert Taylor gave chase. When the thieves saw him coming they dropped it and ran. The police caught them a few days later and the experience worked in our favour in a way, because we were more on our guard.

But security was always a problem, even when Highclere went commercial, though I must say that during the time I was there we had only two books and a leather bookmark stolen. There was, however, one addition. It was still there when I visited the Castle in 2001 and I imagine it remains to this day. In East Anglia dressing room, inside the bedcovers and with its head on the pillow, lies a cuddly toy, brand new. It's been there for several years and no one knows how it arrived. We can only guess that one day a child took it into her heart to give a little comfort. How long it will be there one cannot tell – maybe in another ten years the same person will come back to reclaim it!

Lord and Lady Carnarvon interviewed guides in the smoking room ready for the Castle's first opening. Les Taylor took the chosen guides around the Castle to tell them about its history and the contents. There was a large lamp on the piano in the North Library which he told them was made out of human skin and they all believed him. It was indeed made of some kind of skin, but no one knows any more than that. It now resides upstairs, together with its shade. Everyone thought it very gruesome. In the front hall there is also an elephant's foot which came out of the 6th Earl's study.

The evening before we opened to the public in 1988, the waiting staff received a firm warning. Those serving drinks were not to drink on duty, and those serving food were not to eat in front of the guests.

One of the waitresses serving food looked very tipsy at the end of the evening. After all the guests had departed she bumped down each stair on the main staircase, right down to the bottom, giggling away as she flopped into the saloon.

"You'll get the sack if Sarah or Mary catches you", I said.

"Oh no I won't", she said. "I'm on the food side and they didn't say anything about not drinking the drinks so I'm OK".

At the end of the evening we all celebrated with Veuve Cliquot and pure peach juice. The expertise of all the craftsmen came together to recreate a family home, while there was also considerable assistance from Withers painters and decorators. They all brought Highclere Castle into the commercial era.

The Castle opens to the public

It rained solidly for six weeks when we first opened to the public and everyone said it was the curse of old 'Tut'.

The guides were a special breed and came from far and wide, no doubt attracted by the prestige of working at Highclere Castle. They would gather for a ten-minute briefing and be allocated their first position, ready for the public. Some were more knowledgeable than others. Their ages varied and there was no sex discrimination. You couldn't really say they were in it for the money because the job paid only basic rates. Some guides wanted to better themselves and consequently specialised in certain fields. Jane Robinson, for example, lived and breathed Egyptology. She travelled to Egypt and Cairo to absorb Egyptian lifestyle and culture. Unfortunately, later Jane crossed swords with Adrian, the new Castle manager, and departed Highclere as a result. Naturally they both had their views on how things should be, but in the end there could be only one winner. However, she didn't give up on Egyptology and continued to give talks and seminars on the subject.

Guides are in an unenviable position sometimes, especially when they remain attached to their assigned rooms (which most did) in a country home and business is slow. Even though some were bored, they weren't allowed to show it when the public appeared. I couldn't have been a guide as I wouldn't have been able to stay in one place for so long. Tours were introduced as commercial business progressed, so some guides took on a more varied role, while others felt less confident. There have been guides of many different nationalities at Highclere, though one in particular springs to mind. David

Socks was an American and a fusspot, but he was also a bundle of laughs. He wrote a book on Lady Almina, the 5th Earl of Carnarvon's wife. Having guides from various nationalities was very useful because they spoke languages such as French and German, obviously an asset when accompanying a mixed group of visitors.

Barbara Martin was a very talented guide who also helped out in my department on many occasions. When Chris Andrew, who was the chef at the time, needed help Barbara took over the baking for the tea rooms. From there she graduated to become the Carnarvons' cook at Milford Lake House. Her talents extended to making toys and gifts which were sometimes sold in the Castle shop.

Security was always a problem, with windows left open, etc, so the guides had to be very alert. Some mornings, especially on Sundays, the guides were helpful – or most of them were – when cleaning up after wedding parties the previous evening. Betty Mason, Ann Marsh, Margery Goldsmith and little Margaret Bessant were particularly good in that respect, while some of the others would just walk by with their nose in the air.

I was asked why I was writing about the guides in this book and my reply was quite simple. They are part of the team at Highclere and deserve a mention.

As I mentioned earlier, Tim Howland joined as Castle manager to help Harry Herbert and Chica prepare for public opening. Tim's greatest moment came when the South African cricket team arrived in England for their first tour in many years. It was a one-daymatch – South Africa v Lord Carnarvon's team. Shane Warne was a real star and stayed with Tim as his guest. This special day was held at Highclere Cricket Ground on 23rd June 1994, and Lord Porchester charged the 7th Earl £10,000 for the use of his fields for car parking. This made the 7th Earl fume, as you can well imagine!

Shane Warne gave me his autograph at three in the morning after a dinner held in the Castle Library. He said I'd had a long day and deserved two wishes – what would they be? As the South African team had departed leaving Harry, Tim, Shane and a few of Harry's friends, I asked Shane for two things. First, please could I have his autograph; and secondly, would it be possible for them all to go as I was extremely tired and had another long day ahead of me tomorrow. Shane made an official announcement saying that it was time everyone went home, as Maureen was extremely tired and everyone had had a long day. He gave me a huge hug and a peck on the cheek, Harry did the same and everyone departed. Thank goodness!

Laurence Udell from Mercury Communications met Tim and Harry to see if it would be possible to run a series of team building events at the Castle. This involved Highclere being given a whole new telecommunications system and they also agreed to pay for the conversion and refurbishment of certain rooms to suit their requirements. Various rooms in the Castle were redecorated and converted into semi-permanent conference rooms. The 6th Earl's bedroom suite was converted so once again the Withers were called in to do specialised paintwork.

Mercury Communications also requested the redecoration of the tea rooms within a week. The project was given to Pat and Mike Withers as the rooms had to be ready for a satellite conference with America to be screened live on TV. A friend of Chica's, Cosima McGill, made the curtains. Everything looked splendid as the curtains were hung but what no one at Mercury ever found out was that the material wasn't the one chosen. However, it had to stay put.

To enable Mercury to run their team-building seminars, they installed a complete state of the art telecommunications system, located in the butler's office, with Mercury wiring and telephones installed throughout the Castle. Again, this system had to be in place within a week. It worked perfectly until a couple of years later, when it started to cause problems. Of course, as it wasn't a system that Highclere had actually purchased, it then became 'a can of worms'.

The Mercury conferences included team-building exercises in the park, which meant working late into the evening. When the delegates came back from their team exercise, having completed tasks ranging from rowing across Temple Lake in canoes to trekking up Beacon Hill and across the pheasant pens in the dark, they would be challenged by John Mason, carrying his shotgun and dressed as a gamekeeper. John used to frighten them all half to death, as most of the delegates had little or no experience of the countryside and did not know what to expect. Harry would dress as Lord of the Manor. During these exercises the delegates would come knocking on doors hoping to obtain some of the answers to the questions they had been set. After a while I got wise to this and, with the approval of Laurence Udell, I made some of them do a forfeit. I had the hoovering done in the Castle, logs chopped and carried to rooms to lay fires for the next morning, floors washed and toilets cleaned. I have never enjoyed myself so much! Many was the time I and others bombarded Laurence with Mercury Communications stress balls because he kept us up so late organising the next day's events. We all had a good rapport with everyone on his team, which made life easy all round. Everyone had a great time. One group from Scotland presented me with a first edition Mercury phone card as a thank you gift.

Not everything was as easy. There were a few occasions after we'd opened to the public when I can remember standing up to the 7th Earl, but in a very polite way. One day I saw Richard Morris (Lord Carnavon's agent) and Lord Carnarvon looking at my stretch of garden, which comprised only a lawn and a fence – somewhere to exercise my dog Lady. It had some beautiful hydrangeas down one side which I'd inherited from Francis Reid, one of which was a very rare species. I was suddenly informed that my garden was going to be made into a car park for the guides, and I had only 3 days to take everything out. Now, considering I'd had this stretch of garden for 15 years I thought I was justified in having my say.

On another occasion Lord Carnarvon gave me two days to decide whether to move into the flat above the tea rooms, as they had no one to live there and it had to be occupied for insurance reasons. I went back after two days and said that, having thought it through, I didn't want to move. After living in Stable Cottage for 20 years I again thought I was justified. He obviously didn't like it, but he couldn't force me to move and respected my decision in the end.

Arguments between Mary Brown (of Sarah & Mary Catering) and Robert on the catering front could also be pretty tense. The dining room screen was a regular bone of contention because Mary wanted it out to make more room for tables whereas Robert insisted it should stay where it was because it hid the behind-the-scenes debris. The point was, these were commercial caterers, out to make money from their business. Robert knew only domestic life and the private home. It was Robert who actually asked me back to be Francis Reid's assistant in taking care of the house. We were allies, because commercialism had come into our lives and we weren't sure how to handle it. During the time when Sarah & Mary were catering they brought with them their own butler, Mr Victor Kennedy. Although he was a good butler, the 7th Earl didn't take to him for some reason. But he had great influence on my son Chris's life. In my 32 years at the Castle I experienced five different butlers at work.

I always felt that the 7th Earl never expected me to run Highclere with the catering companies or Harry and Chica, the main reason being that I was a woman. His generation had always dealt with butlers and valets. He already had a butler at Milford Lake House, John Stratford, who at one time had worked for the 6th Earl as a chauffeur. (John's wife Kath cooked for both Earls.) Mr Clifford, a butler/valet, also helped at Milford Lake and had known the 7th Earl during his army days as a valet. Sometimes Mr Clifford came to Highclere for functions after the previous butler Robert Taylor passed away.

Following the end of Sarah and Mary's catering contract at Highclere Castle, the family chose Crown Catering as their successors and they catered for us for three years. This arrangement wasn't without its difficulties, however. On one occasion during Crown's term at Highclere their van coming to us from London was involved in an accident and didn't arrive in time for lunch. As we had an event taking place at the Castle and lunch was of great importance, what could we do? I immediately took charge, removed all the chicken from my freezer, defrosted it and starting to cook. I barked out orders to the kitchen porter and between us we solved the problem. While all of this was going on a tour was organised to buy us a bit more time. Crown Catering turned up after lunch without a word of apology. I think they were probably quite put out to think that we'd turned a possible disaster into a triumph! Crown had so many close calls because of the distance they travelled from London that when Lord Porchester's (later the 8th Earl's) shooting party nearly had to go to the Yew Tree for lunch it was decided to employ in-house chefs.

It was not only catering which was a potential problem. During the 6th Earl's time, most of the flower arranging was done by Mr Alexander, a local florist from Boki's flower shop in Newbury. The gardens were still tended by the Castle gardeners. As the Castle became more of a commercial enterprise, large floral arrangements were gradually dispensed with and more houseplants appeared. The first year of opening to the public, dried flowers were used in the bedrooms, but that proved unsuccessful and the 7th Countess of Carnarvon decided to use potted plants instead.

Scented geraniums were a useful plant and could be mixed with standard lemon trees in the corner of the saloon. To a housekeeper, though, they were a total nightmare when they were in flower as the flowers dropped everywhere, but they were beautiful, especially when the scent greeted you first thing in the morning as you opened the shutters. Firm favourites of the 7th Earl were the beautiful jasmine trees gracing the rooms in early spring. Stephanosis came later with its exquisite scent and then wonderful orchids were brought into the house from Covent Garden. The 7th Earl and Countess loved white and pastel shades, unlike the 6th Earl, who favoured darker colours. Ann Marsh, among many others, excelled at flower arranging and often combined it with her duties as a guide at the Castle. Ann was one of our head guides and a friend whom I could talk to. Many times during my troubles she'd say: "Remember, Maureen, engage brain before opening mouth and count to ten".

During the shooting season small trees called Tibouchina were put in the front hall. They were lovely but had to go because when they flowered they dropped on to the marble and stained it. During weddings, flowers cascaded over the front entrance, down the pillars in the entrance hall and also down the staircase. Many florists understood perfectly well what was required but others had no idea and were soon put right. For a while rose petals became popular at weddings, scattered on the tables and making a trail for the bride's entrance before the marriage, but they soon lost their appeal because of the damage done to the carpets.

Table arrangements for functions were also initially by Boki's but then it became Ann Marsh's duty to organise them for commercial weddings and functions as they were part and parcel of the financial package. With Adrian Wiley's arrival as Castle manager, a new regime began which cut the cost of flowers for the dining tables at weddings and left them looking just as effective. Tall glass vases with sprays of tall lilies were sometimes used. They were wonderfully simple, but sometimes the lilies were either out too far or in bud and then heat lamps had to be used to try to make them look perfect on the bride's big day. Sometimes this worked and sometimes it didn't.

Highclere as a commercial venture

CONFERENCES AND EVENTS AT HIGHCLERE

There was an occasion when I turned Bill Gates, head of Microsoft, out of the back State Rooms. Everyone was in a conference called 'Experience through the Gates of Microsoft'. Well, I'd never heard of Bill Gates but he shouldn't have been walking around the State Rooms because they were off limits to the conference. He didn't look like anyone who might own a huge business as he had long hair and wore jeans and sweatshirt with a crumpled jacket. How was I to know how important he was? It was the first time we'd run such a large conference in the Library, with 280 people, an activity day and then dinner as part of the event. I explained the situation to him and for a change I was very tactful and courteous – then someone told me who he was. I apologised to him and we had a good laugh about it; he was a very nice person to talk to and very easy going. I offered him a tour of the Egyptian artefacts as a way of saying sorry and he accepted.

IBM had a conference at Highclere to demonstrate voice to computer technology. No expense was spared and they had a U-shaped table made especially for the Library for this event. The delegates were flown in by helicopter and Gary Singer and his wife offered me a job in America. I sent the following letter in reply:

'Three significant occasions have made 1996 stand out as a year that will always be remembered. The enclosed film was a lot of fun and we are hoping they will make a series of it. The publicity created enormous media

interest which has got to be beneficial to Highclere. It also comes as quite a surprise to be recognised by so many of our visitors!

Another treat this year had been meeting both The Queen and Queen Mother in the Castle. Although The Queen has often been to the estate she has never had a tour before.

The third occasion came about through your very kind offer to recruit me after twenty-eight years at Highclere. It was very flattering as well as tempting to pursue a new career in the States. After much consideration, I very much regret that I shall not be able to join you on account of my love for Highclere.

I appreciate your kind consideration and look forward to welcoming you to the Castle again in the not too distant future".

Other special events that have been held at Highclere include functions for BMW, Porsche and Rolls Royce who all used the fantastic setting as a background to launch their new cars.

Over the past few years the Southern Counties Fair has grown into an enormous event. Tony Scutt, principal organiser with help from his brother Roger, made me feel part of things as soon as they arrived. They made me one of the family and have done so ever since. Among the celebrities who attended the show was Katie Cropper, the only shepherdess to have won One Man and his Dog. She was always bubbly and full of fun. John Craven came from BBC TV's Newsround to interview her. She was a great personality to have at the Fair. Another celebrity who enjoyed the event was Pam St. Clement, alias Pat Butcher from East Enders. She was a lovely lady, perfectly at ease with everyone and great to talk to.

On one occasion Tony Scutt had a very unusual request. Apparently he suffered from sore testicles and was in a great deal of pain, due to the many miles he'd walked around the show organising events. He asked if he could have a bath in the Castle to alleviate the problem. Well, my personal view was that he should have the best chilled champagne, Handel's choral music, a cigar, a large salt bath with a warm, extra-large towel complete with two duck decoys. He was ecstatic and the pain gradually eased, which made him a very happy man.

Another event that has been carefully looked after for many years takes place every August Bank Holiday. The event in question is the Highclere Horse Trials and the organiser is Janet Benney, whose enthusiasm and determination have made the event the success it is today. The kindness that her whole family has shown me is second to none, from her husband Gerald – still one of the leading goldsmiths of the age and former goldsmith to The Queen – to their son Simon, who has followed in his father's footsteps. Gerald, incidentally, is the only craftsman ever to have won all four Royal Warrants together. Another son, Paul Benney, a world-famous artist who painted Jerry Hall, Mick Jaggers ex-wife, amongst others, welcomed me into his London home as if he'd known me for years. I was pleased to help both Gerald and Simon with their exhibitions at Allerton Castle in 1999 – before it burned down – and in their shop at Walton Street, South Kensington. It is an honour to have been part of their lives. A special moment came when they gave me a superb gold goblet in return for all my hard work. It will be treasured by me and my family for years to come. Thank you. Of course, I must not forget to mention Jonathon, their third son, who is a very talented furniture restorer.

AN ASIDE – HELICOPTERS

My love of helicopters was born when the Southern Counties Fair arrived at Highclere and one of the attractions was a helicopter ride – £15 for 10 minutes. My first ride was complimentary and then you could not keep me away. I was actually frightened to fly in a helicopter, one of the reasons being the uncertainty of it all. In fact, I was scared to death. Finally I plucked up courage and oh, my, what an exhilarating experience. Thereafter, I was known as 'Chopper Cummins'. Whenever I had the chance I would be up in the sky soaring overhead and seeing things I had only dreamt about.

I would travel around the Castle whenever shots were needed for Channel 4's 'Return to Egypt', with Lord Porchester (now the 8th Earl) walking around his grandfather's grave, which is situated on Beacon Hill.

With Adrian and Lindsey I flew down the new A34 by-pass, just before it opened, to celebrate 30 years at Highclere. This was a present to myself and to say thank you to two wonderful people. We were starting a new business venture at Ardington House, so I had organised the trip to fly around and get an aerial view. How magnificent and beautiful it all was. Adrian's door came open and, as he was in front, we thought he was larking about. Apparently not; he was really scared and told us so in no uncertain terms. The pilot apologised for the incident.

On my 50th birthday I received a twenty-minute lesson to give me an idea of how difficult it is to fly. I was over the moon and could not have received a better present from my friends.

I shall always be fascinated and exhilarated by helicopters. The world looks different from the air and the experience gives you freedom of thought, tranquillity and a buzz of excitement and joy. My future aim is not to learn to fly but just to enjoy every moment up there while I can. If anyone needs a passenger, please contact me; I am always happy to help out.

My present also included a journey in a stretch limo with a few friends to a casino for an evening meal and lots of fun. What a shame no one thought to take any photographs. It was a memorable evening and the look on my face when I saw the limo will never be forgotten. My grateful thanks to everyone; I felt very special and had a wonderful time. I even won nearly £100, but when I came back from the ladies' room Adrian had lost it all! I was dumbfounded, but he did give it all back to me the next day.

STRIFE IN AND AROUND THE CASTLE

My obsession with Highclere was a commitment that lasted 32 years, the fulfilment of a dream if you like. But I've gone out into the big wide world now and realise I should have done so a long, long time ago. Often enough my devotion to Highclere caused extreme aggravation. There were heated discussions as a result of my blinkered approach to how things should be done and my very high standards. Often I simply failed to understand why other people couldn't see my point of view.

I remember a time when Harry took some filming people around the Castle for a movie to be made at Highclere. We lost the contract because of the state of the rooms. Renovation of a new room to accommodate the Racing Exhibition was in progress and the dust and dirt came through the floorboards in the dining room, the front hall and the Library. I didn't realise it had gone everywhere. I was blamed and Harry hauled me over the coals. I swore then that the Castle would always look sparkling and we'd never lose business for a similar reason again. My staff lost faith in me because of my attitude and sometimes reported me to the manager (later Adrian Wiley) because they felt that repetition of some of the work simply wasn't necessary. Even my friend Lindsey Giles couldn't see my point of view. I tried to explain to her that that was how I'd been taught, just as she was taught high standards when working on the computer or typing. My attitude was, if something wasn't clean and spotless, how could business be generated?

Mark, the chef at that time, had standards but my department was the first to be seen and it was important to create a warm and welcoming atmosphere. I was a hands-on housekeeper and found it hard to delegate because I could get the job done faster by myself. Later, as we became busier, I found this much harder and ended up wearing myself out most of the time. Gradually work was farmed out to other departments and I felt I was no longer required and on the scrap heap, left with all the menial jobs to do. This gradually brought on depression and, together with the unsatisfactory nature of my home life, meant that I stayed more and more at the Castle, where my office became my home. I only went to Stable Cottage to sleep.

This prompted certain members of staff to think I had something to hide, a feeling encouraged by the fact that I also kept my office locked all the time. Some of them thought I didn't do all that much anyway. I started under-estimating myself and sank into depression. Needing to be wanted and to be told honestly about things wasn't that much to ask, I felt.

Mary Povey used to say that I should spend more time with Chris, watching him grow up, so when I could I arranged for him to help me at the Castle at weekends or during the holidays. I paid him until he was of an age to be paid by the Castle. He became a guide and helped as a waiter. What Mary hadn't realised was that I was the one keeping a roof over our heads. However, I hadn't seen that my obsession with Highclere would cause a rift between my son and me and not create the bond I'd hoped for. It seemed I'd have an uphill struggle to stay as close to Highclere as I wanted.

Quite often my obsession clouded my judgment and I was wary of giving the tiniest piece of information to anyone. I was afraid that one day I wouldn't be needed and all my love for Highclere would count for nothing. At home, people generally have photographs of their family on display but not me. Nearly all of my photos, and there were hundreds, were of Highclere at different times of year, in all kinds of weather and from a variety of angles. I rose early just to get certain pictures. I spent hours on the roof or tower just surveying the surroundings, watching the deer in the woods or enjoying the peace and tranquillity of my Highclere. There was always something different to look at and you could see for miles around, especially on a clear day.

I found that I had very little in common with people. But I was a good listener, I loved to mother them and give them my whole attention and make them feel special. I preferred to stand back and not be at the centre of things, especially if important people were around. As long as people appreciated what I did, that was fine with me. I cared. Perhaps I should have been more dynamic and pushed myself more. The problem was, I didn't know how. I needed direction. I'm a practical person, not a business person, and at least I was aware of it.

The truth is, my whole life revolved around Highclere. Over the years it destroyed my relationship with friends, ruled out going to dances and other social events, and generally distanced me from the outside world. Eventually, when we opened on a commercial basis, I had to spend more time establishing a rapport with guests at functions, which was time consuming. When I did take a holiday I was always homesick by Wednesday and couldn't wait to get back to work. My life, my world, everything about me revolved around Highclere. It was my safe haven – like being cocooned in a time capsule. I was afraid to do anything else or have hobbies like normal people.

There was so much to be involved in, especially when the commercial side started up, that I felt my total commitment was all that mattered. I recall coming back from holiday in midweek on one occasion when we had an important American dinner on and it was essential that everything was in tip-top condition. On my return in late afternoon I saw that someone had lit the fire in the Library but omitted to put the chimney hatch up so you couldn't see anything for smoke. Quickly relaying instructions to open the Library windows – as I recall it was a September evening with a nip in the air, which is why the fire was lit – we managed to rectify the situation.

Time was moving on and the guests were due for a drinks reception in the Library. Panic rose instead of air freshener but, by the time they arrived, the Library was back to normal. There was a faint whiff of smoke, which the Americans loved, a warm welcome and a successful dinner to look forward to. My neck was in the noose with Tony because I couldn't get back to the West Country until the next day but to me the effort was worthwhile. Everyone thought I was crazy, especially Les Taylor, because I'd given up holiday time again but I felt deep satisfaction and above all everything had gone well. That's how committed I was.

I had problems with Chica and Harry, when they took over the running of the Castle from Lord Porchester. Chica had convinced Lord Carnarvon that she could handle the catering. For six years we had used contract caterers and now Lord Carnarvon wanted his own cook or chef. Chica, who was a food consultant for Marks & Spencer, took over the cooking herself but found it was very demanding and eventually formed a team of cooks to handle the catering while she looked after the department upstairs and the tea rooms.

Ann Collins, formerly a cleaner in my department, had put in for the position of head waitress while I was having days off and been offered the position. Little did I know that this would change my life yet again. As time went on, so Ann and Chica gradually built up a wall between themselves and me. They were trying to extract information about how the dining room was run in the old days but I could see little point in telling them because, in my opinion, there was a considerable difference between running a family home and operating a commercial enterprise. Life became a battleground again and friction was inevitable. My son Chris was very popular with Harry and Chica because he was on Ann's team and they felt that, as a man, he was the ideal person to greet guests. He was kitted out with a morning suit so that he could take on the role. You can imagine my reaction. Up until then this had been my job, but now I was being made to feel that I just wasn't good enough. As I was from the north my accent was considered unsuitable, so Chris became Harry's right hand man when it came to greeting guests.

Given that I was working harder because of the extra functions, life at home wasn't too special and Chris had put my nose out of joint. As I persevered and kept fighting for my rights as housekeeper, my knowledge was called upon yet again because I'd been at Highclere for so long. Harry and Chica both wanted me to help Ann Collins and couldn't understand why I wouldn't co-operate.

If Ann had had any idea of the way we went about things in a country house I might have been more approachable, but all her experience was in pubs and hotels.

Harry and Chica were trying to encourage a homely, relaxed atmosphere at Highclere but, at the same time, run it along commercial lines. They even thought of bringing in waiters from South Africa, where they'd recently been on holiday, to give the Castle more prestige as they'd been so impressed with the service they'd received. As time went on they had their first, and last, medieval banquet in the saloon for a computer company based in Basingstoke. The waitress staff all had to dress up in period costume. The average age was 25 and they'd all come for a fun evening out. They'd already had drinks on the coaches before arriving at Highclere and their behaviour was boisterous. Fruit and rolls were thrown around during the banquet and valuable paintings were pelted with food – they had absolutely no respect for their surroundings. C4 was producing the programme *High Stakes at Highclere* at the time and they were over the moon with the company's bad behaviour because it made for good television.

My marriage undoubtedly suffered because of my obsession with Highclere. Without my knowing it Laura Martin, daughter of Barbara Martin, a former guide, had become rather friendly with Tony, my husband, and was spending a lot of time at our house. She and Tony had formed a special relationship which caused quite a lot of rows, so I stayed at work even more. As I was under a lot of pressure both at work and at home, life had very little meaning and the hours I worked became longer and longer.

Ann Collins had been to see Chica to try and get me removed as I was a thorn in her side and she wanted complete control of the front of house, dining room and tea rooms. I was summoned to a meeting with Chica and Lady Carnarvon to go over the problems and see how they might be resolved. I remained cool, calm and in control but with a temper simmering like a volcano about to erupt. After the meeting Lady Carnarvon found me in tears in the servery and put an arm around me, saying: "I agree with you, Maureen, but I really can't support you because Chica is my daughter-in-law".

I was about to go to Austria for my holiday. All I wanted was to get away and my mind was in total turmoil. Holidays weren't much fun anyway, because Tony sat smoking and watching the world go by from our balcony, while Chris watched cartoons on satellite TV all day. I walked up the mountain as there didn't seem much else to do. Battling with my emotions, with no one to talk to and feeling really down and depressed, I actually considered walking off the mountain and committing suicide – that would solve everything. Tony could go with Laura, Ann Collins could run the Castle and I'd be at peace.

Of course, this didn't happen but I did decide to write what turned out to be an important letter to my friend Lindsey. It got me help from the doctor and life began to look a little better. Laura went to see her aunt in America, met someone later on and finally emigrated. She wrote constantly to Tony until she went away. He never forgave me for breaking up their relationship and things were never the same between us. Chica employed Chris Andrews a chef because she could no longer cope with the stress and strain of running the catering operation and Harry, whose horse racing syndicate business had taken off, handed over the management reins at Highclere to his partner Tim Howland.

I was still there, looking after clients during functions, and Chris and I gradually came to tolerate each other. Ann Collins kept out of my way.

ADRIAN WILEY COMES TO HIGHCLERE

Sadly, Tim Howland was offered a position organising a large event abroad and was poached from under our noses! As Harry's horseracing syndicate interests were growing and he could not devote sufficient time to running the Castle, Adrian Wiley – the 'ticketyboo' man – was appointed.

Unbeknown to any of us Adrian had been around Highclere before. A couple of years previously he had attended an Historic House Association meeting and had already done the rounds. The first that anyone knew of his arrival was when John Mason remarked that his friend from Performing Arts (a concert company) had had dealings with Adrian before. His most celebrated saying was: 'Everything is ticketyboo'. Many of us involved with the Castle did not understand him when he arrived. Also, I hated the thought that he might take things away from me. Yet again we would have to go back to basics, with all the aggravation that involved. Life was far from simple and I did not want everything turned upside down again.

Tim, Harry and Chica had always left me to meet and greet guests, organise the staff and run functions when they went home. If you've ever seen *High Stakes at Highclere*, you'll know how much I disapproved of the changeover. You can see in the film how much I hated Adrian Wiley and how I just about managed to put up with the daily routine, thinking how hard done by I was. I thought I could change him and said as much. Many a time I thought, what planet does this man come from?

Finally, after months of aggression and near hatred at having my world turned upside down, I watched the recording of the programme. Everyone gave him such a hard time – the guides, the staff and I – that it was a wonder he did not give us all the sack! I know I was very close. My attitude towards him was very vindictive and we had many cross words, mainly because my approach was wrong. 'Listen, house manager! I'm the housekeeper and you'd better not forget it', that was the way I went about things. But what did I know about managing anything anyway? Converting me to his way of thinking must have been his worst nightmare.

Many times I was told that I was guilty of causing unrest among the staff. This was because I thought of myself as the person in charge but now I had to put up with Adrian Wiley wanting to do things his way. The saga when a washing-up machine was installed downstairs caused a lot of resentment among staff because we had to carry dirty dishes all the way downstairs, from the servery to the tea rooms, where before we had always washed up by hand in the servery. It was common sense to do this as we were busy and the noise of the machine could be heard inside the dining room. In the end all hell broke loose because it was a long haul to the tea rooms and back again. You had to be careful because it was always difficult to get regular staff and many of them were travelling long distances to work at that time.

I was very arrogant and not all of my complaints were justified. The Carnarvons were pussycats compared to Adrian Wiley! I felt my loyalties were to the Carnarvons and he'd better not forget it – he and his high and mighty ways. Who did he think he was, anyway? As I discovered later, it was his tact and diplomacy (qualities I lacked) which slowly converted the guides, the staff and me to a more businesslike way of going about things. I did not know anything about the business world, my whole life had been dedicated to Highclere and to looking after what I loved, cared for and wanted to protect. As I saw it, this man Adrian was a definite threat to me when he arrived and I always gave my opinion with no holds barred, especially when I thought the old way of doing things was about to disappear. On one occasion, when I heard discussions about ripping out the plate warmer in the server, my hackles rose. "To what purpose?" I asked. "It's part of our heritage, you can't do that'. In his tactful way he said it could remain; I'm sure the whole debate was engineered to wind me up. It must have taken him a while to get me on the straight and narrow, as I was always prepared to oppose him.

I wasn't the only one to have a confrontational attitude towards Adrian during the first few months of his reign. The guides also rebelled against him and the new ideas he tried to put into practice. Visitors coming through the Georgian entrance (the back door) became a major issue – the Carnarvons argued against it, though they were willing to support a trial run. But the guides petitioned much more strongly against the idea and disagreed wholeheartedly with Adrian. They were so adamant that a threat to walk out reached the Carnarvons' ears. Eventually a discussion between all parties led to the decision to revert to the front entrance. So, this was one battle that Adrian didn't win, though it was more a question of the Carnarvons deciding to leave things as they were than the guides forcing the issue.

Peace reigned once again. Ancient Egypt became part of the national curriculum in schools, so guides began organising tours of the Egyptian Room for schoolchildren. Later, as the subject became even more popular, the old brush room was converted to a 'hands on' room to educate the children further, taking them back in time by dressing them up in Egyptian costumes, hats and jewellery. Highclere was, after all, the main centre for Egyptology as it was the home of the 5th Earl, who financed the excavation in the first place.

I always fought, without success, for staff breaks and meals after working long hours, but things improved when the Statute for Working Rules and Regulations came into effect. After a few months of Adrian's reign at Highclere Castle, I received a letter from him. 'Oh my God, I've had it now, I've got my notice', I thought, but it wasn't that at all, it was confirmation that I'd been upgraded to house manager. Well, this totally confused me because I was a housekeeper and proud of it. I wrote him a letter telling him what I thought of him, which would make very interesting reading now! But, when I look back, I wonder if my staff appreciated or even realised what I did for them and how much trouble I got into on their behalf. I suppose they remember the bad things about me, not the good. Reluctantly, I took on the job of house manager. I stated from the outset that I had not received any proper training when it came to looking after staff or running functions because I always did what came naturally. Of course, this did not go down well. Eventually I lost confidence in myself and was afraid to ask anything, as I never seemed to get anywhere when I did.

My way of life and going about things slowly changed. I still voiced my opinions, but in a different way. Some of my responsibilities were passed on to other people as we became busier and busier, and some of the tension ebbed away. It was not easy when Adrian Wiley first arrived but we lived to fight another day! In 1998, with the granting of a wedding licence, a banqueting manager was employed to take the pressure off me and other members of staff. Respect slowly grew for Adrian, this man who had invaded my life, and a mutual understanding developed between us. To see him run the hoover over carpets and floors, help put furniture back after functions ready for another event or, when the Castle was open to the public, put ropes and posts back and develop a relationship with staff after hours, helped enormously.

Perhaps we ought to sort something out at this stage. My intense dislike for Adrian Wiley turned to admiration and respect, many people thought I loved him. Well, it was never like that, but a sort of hero worship developed. Adrian brought things into my life that I had never dreamed of. He burst the bubble I'd been cocooned in for 25 years and broadened my outlook. He developed my skills and brought me into the 20th Century, stimulating my brain in a way I never thought possible. We became a team. He had this way of making everyone feel special. He gave freely of himself, bringing warmth, charm, generosity and laughter into his dealings with people. All I can say is that he made me happier than I had ever been, and his friendship went far beyond anything that money could buy. Yes, he could be a hard taskmaster, but he had a way with words that meant people would do anything for him. And, of course, he was a talented businessman. He put Highclere on the map commercially, privately and as a stately home. That is why it is so surprising – and unreasonable – that Lord and Lady Carnarvon never appreciated him. Let's not forget he took Highclere out of the red and into the black (Lady Carnarvon's own words to me), turning it into a profitable venture along the way.

Adrian developed our skills and made us all into management material. He pointed out something that no one had ever bothered with before, that my job was as important as others. He appreciated that I was a person and not a servant – something the Carnarvons had forgotten, I think. My opinions counted and I was part of the old way of life which he did not want to lose. Many times I felt there was no appreciation of what I did from the Carnarvons – especially the 7th Earl! But I got myself so worried and worked up that I actually made myself ill, because Highclere was my whole world. I felt that I was on trial and I was unsure of what was required of me. I felt Lindsey and I were facing the unknown, whereas the other members of the team seemed confident and unconcerned because they had all worked on commercial events before.

THE STAFF IN MY DEPARTMENT AT HIGHCLERE CASTLE

PHILIP AND LINDA MAHONEY

Philip and Linda came to work for me about a year after the Castle opened to the public but only stayed a few months as they'd always worked outside and couldn't adjust to an inside job. Philip always kept looking at his watch, even in front of the 7th Earl. Lord Carnarvon hated this and was therefore very pleased to see him go.

TIM AND MAUREEN O'MAHONEY

Tim and Maureen were my next employees and they stayed for three years. Their first day involved Tim sitting on the loo only to find hot water gushing up from the water system. They were Irish and good hard workers but it all got too much for them after Tim had an operation on his leg and had to retire through ill health.

RICHARD AND JULIE HEATH

Richard and Julie were a wonderful couple but, as we got busier, they became very discontented. Richard had a famous saying. When asked how they were, his response was: "Poor but happy". We had a few laughs, though. Richard always had the Saturday Telegraph and never liked anyone to read it before he did. I always liked The Times or Telegraph on a Saturday so I'd have a quick look first. He then handed over the whole paper on Monday. On their arrival at Highclere we had a great storm and poor Julie went into her sitting room and the whole ceiling fell on top of her, rain and everything. They had to move into other rooms (the upstairs tea rooms) to live while it was repaired. They were so much in love that they went everywhere together, sometimes on their bikes. It was lovely to see, and a very sad day when they left Highclere after 5 years.

CHRIS AND MANDY MARFLEET

Chris and Mandy initially came to Highclere to work for me as cleaners and I thought they were a very pleasant couple. They were both very ambitious and managed to get themselves upgraded from cleaning staff to banqueting staff. But I hadn't realised how intense internal politics could be. This was almost like a war and I felt I was constantly battling to safeguard my own position. Quite a lot of it was my own fault as I didn't want to relinquish my influence and status at the Castle. Battle followed battle and I could never see eye to eye with them until the point was reached where they no longer wanted to work for me. They were always running to Lord and Lady Carnarvon and complaining about me without airing their grievances with Adrian first.

When they were first at Highclere my son, Chris, ran both the bar at the cricket pitch on match days and the bar inside the Castle at events. Mandy accused him of being light-fingered and, although he was old enough to stick up for himself, I was angered by the way he was treated and belittled. I always kept large sums of money at home as I didn't have a bank account until I was nearly 50, and nothing had ever had gone missing. Chris, unjustly accused, lost faith in everyone and – being his mother's son – took immediate action and left. This gave me a big problem because I had to choose whom to support – my son or Adrian Wiley, my boss, who had gone along with the accusation. To be loyal to Highclere Castle and Adrian was very difficult at times. There were many occasions when I felt I'd failed my son and this is one I'll always regret, rightly or wrongly.

After Chris's departure, Chris Marfleet took over the running of both bars. I cannot forget those times or forgive what happened to my son and I could

h Earl pictured in the horse racing museum room at Highclere

Lady Carolyn's wedding to John Warren

Geordie Herbert's wedding to Jane Wilby, 1989,
HM The Queen and HRH Princess Margaret with the family group
David Hartley Photographs

ordie Herbert and Jane Wilby on their wedding day

d Hartley Photographs

The Hon. Harry Herbert's wedding to Chica, 1992,
HM The Queen and HRH Princess Diana with the family group

HM The Queen and HRH Princess and the Carnarvons at the The Hon. Harry Herbert's wedding to Chica, 1992

Christening of John and Lady Carolyn Warren's ch
at Highclere Chur

Carnarvon family Christmas card

Maureen and the
Countess of Carnarvon
inspecting worn curtains, 1995

Publicity shot for *High Stakes at Highclere*, 1996 (Maureen on middle left)
Thanks to Maria Noble and Channel 4

taff at Highclere, Maureen on left towards the back

His Lordship's done WHAT?? -
Adrian Wiley in serious mode

Adrian (centre) in less serio
mode as Lord Carnarvo
presents Tony Scutt with t
Trim Memorial Cup f
sheepdog tria

The Three Musketeers - Bill Porritt,
Jack Rolfe and Adrian after a
fishing expedition

Bill Porritt and his partner Sandy McCa

never really understand why the Marfleets changed from the pleasant people they seemed to be in the early days. It was a long time before I forgave Adrian for the cricket incident. Quite often cricket teams ran a tab and forgot to pay, so the receipts didn't tally. Phil Frogley and Chris used to lark about but they were young and inexperienced, certainly not dishonest. They both ran the cricket bar, but only Chris was accused. Chris was still at university at the time and his world expanded when he left Highclere. Moving on was a good thing for him.

DIANA MOYSE

The most loyal, dedicated and diligent person I ever had working for me was Diana Moyse. She saw me through many trials and tribulations. She wasn't ambitious and always said she hated cleaning but was excellent at it. She loved to be told what to do without realising that she was perfectly capable of being housekeeper at Highclere Castle herself. She was the only person I felt I could confide in and to whom I could pass on my knowledge. She would probably hate it if she knew that I had written about her. She is a wonderful friend and I left Highclere knowing that she would use my knowledge wisely.

THE CARNARVONS IN THE COMMERICAL PERIOD

I was always wary of the 7th Earl, especially after he reported me to the Castle manager for using his loo. Adrian had me on the carpet (not for the first time) and told me all my failings. But everyone had used the loo since the Castle opened commercially. The guides even christened it 'the guides' loo'. However, I must give the 7th Earl his due; he did look after me when I was very ill. He had me rushed to a private hospital and paid all the bills. Lady Carnarvon had a great deal of influence in the matter.

During the 7th Earl's time at Highclere, and especially during the shooting season, I'd be at the front door meeting and greeting people, a job I loved. I would greet guests with a warm smile and a hearty "Good morning!" although this was toned down when the 7th Earl arrived, depending on whether he had a scowl on his face or looked in a jovial mood. On shoots I'd put the 7th Earl's shuffles out so that he wouldn't have to take his shoes off and the dirt would remain inside the shuffle. (Shuffles were large flat slippers that were worn over boots or shoes.) If, however, he was in a bad mood or the shoot wasn't going as expected he would walk straight in, clay, mud and everything on his boots and storm straight to the Gents toilet leaving his dirty footprints all over the beautiful carpets. He'd then change his shoes after lunch. Believe me, this made me as mad as hell and I'm sure he did it just to wind me up.

Over the years various moneymaking opportunities have been missed for one reason or another. Andrew Lloyd Webber bought, through his 'Trust', four Holy Grail tapestries by Sir Edward Burne Jones and William Morris. In 1999 these pre-Raphaelite tapestries were supposed to come to Highclere. They would have been perfect, placed around the balustrades. Andrew Lloyd Webber was thrilled that at long last he had somewhere to display these wonderful works of art. People from Hampton Court came to check for light, moisture and positioning. Everything was in place for the arrival of the tapestries which offered Highclere a rare and wonderful opportunity. Lord Lloyd Webber came over from Sydmonton and had meetings with the 7th Earl. The deal was nearly done and the tapestries would have a home until 2004, at which point it was intended to display the pre-Raphaelites and other Masters at the Royal Academy of Arts in London. As things turned out, the exhibition actually took place between 20 September and 12 December 2003 and was well worth the wait.

The reason Highclere completely missed out was that suddenly, right out of the blue, the 7th Earl changed his mind and everything was cancelled. The income from visitors would have been enormous. Some say it was because the impresario had opposed his application for a golf course at Ridgemoor Farm in Burghclere and this was his way of retaliating. Who knows? But the fact is that the 7th Earl had allowed personal feelings to come before the welfare of Highclere: I overheard the 7th Earl say after Andrew Lloyd Webber had left: "I really don't like that man, and I don't trust him".

For the Millennium it was decided by the 7th Earl and management that the Castle would not open on a commercial basis owing to the cost involved. The Carnarvons celebrated the Millennium on top of Beacon Hill with the Bishop of Winchester, the vicar of Highclere, a few dedicated followers plus Les Taylor, a few mince pies, a blazing fire and a rocket. We, the staff, spent the Millennium with our families at the Newbury Manor Hotel, wining, dining and partying well into the early hours. It was a fun occasion and life was definitely for the living as we entered a new century. What a party we had!

There was an occasion when the Bolshoi Ballet had been booked to perform at Highclere Castle. Highclere was responsible for the ticket sales so, when someone absconded with the money, probably to Ireland, not only from our estate but from others as well, the 7th Earl was responsible for repaying all the ticket sales – a sum in the region of £25,000. He paid up because Highclere Castle had to maintain its reputation.

Lady Jane and Geordie (then Lord Porchester) got on the wrong side of the 7th Earl when they became involved in a pyramid company called Amway, selling American cleaning products. He strongly objected to their using the Castle as a backdrop for a photo shoot in Hello! magazine. The mere idea of being associated 'with trade'! Little did he know what was to follow.

DEMPSTER AND THE 7th EARL

Lady Carnarvon produced a second cookbook in which I was fortunate enough to have some of my recipes recorded for posterity. When the book was launched at the Four Seasons Hotel in London, Jennifer Paterson (one of the Two Fat Ladies from BBC TV), who arrived clad in motor cycle attire, discovered that Lady Carnarvon's chocolate pot recipe was, in fact, one of her own. Jennifer seemed truly delighted that her recipe had given so much pleasure to so many people over the years. It was at this book launch that people also realised what an intense dislike the 7th Earl felt for another of the guests, gossip columnist Nigel Dempster.

Over the years Nigel had never missed an opportunity to have a go at the Earl in his famous column in the *Daily Mail*. I remember on one occasion, when we hosted breakfast at the Castle before a race meeting, back in the days of Sarah & Mary Catering, the 7th Earl behaved very curtly towards him in the saloon. Dempster had been particularly unfair when Lord Carnarvon gave a speech in the House of Lords, fully endorsing the proposed Newbury by-pass, which anyone who used the old road knew was absolutely essential. The Earl eloquently made the point that the route through the middle of his estate was the only single carriageway between Southern Spain and Scotland! Dempster made no reference to this in his column but concentrated instead on the seven-figure sum the 7th Earl would receive for selling two acres of land in order to build what is now Tot Hill Services. Needless to say, Dempster had his facts all wrong because it was Lord Porchester who owned the land and therefore benefited handsomely from the deal. The 7th Earl had no time at all for the columnist after that.

THE AFFAIR OF FIONA'S DOG

You will appreciate that the popular press generally, not just Nigel Dempster, took great interest in the goings-on at Highclere and we needed to be on our guard.

Fiona, the present 8th Countess of Carnarvon, married the 8th Earl quietly in the Savoy chapel when he was still Lord Porchester. The occasion had none of the grandeur of Geordie's first marriage to Jane Wilby, now Jane, Lady Porchester, which was attended by Her Majesty The Queen and Princess Margaret. In taking Fiona's hand in marriage he had also taken on a mongrel that Fiona was besotted with but which actually belonged to her previous boyfriend, Sir Ben Slade. This cross between a Doberman pincher and black Labrador had inherited, from one of Sir Ben's aged aunts, the sum of £50,000 – a considerable amount for a human being, never mind a dog. Sir Ben was incandescent with rage at losing Fiona's heart and pursued his dog through the law courts. We all had to write letters for Geordie to produce in court, supporting his and Fiona's claim.

As you can well imagine, the story of the mongrel's 'abduction' turned into a media extravaganza and took up two pages in the News of the World, with the national dailies all showing plenty of interest as well. The battle continued for some considerable time until judgement was made against Fiona, with costs running into five figures. Also, the dog had to be returned. He was a star by now and featured in the television programme Pampered Pets. All in all, his profile had been raised to the point where his media value was estimated at around £130,000.

Incidentally, Lord Porchester and Fiona decided to live at Highclere. Naturally enough, she didn't want to reside in the same house as his previous wife, so the decision was taken to move to Field House, where his brother Harry and family lived. You can imagine the storm that broke between the two brothers, especially as Harry and Chica had spent thousands renovating the house and offices for their home and business next door, Highclere Thoroughbred Racing. In the end it cost Geordie more than £200,000 to evict his brother, wife and family. Eventually Highclere Thoroughbred Racing moved offices, thereby accommodating Fiona's clothing business Azur

TEAMBUILDING

Our teambuilding sessions began in the study at Highclere Castle. Highclere was run on a lot of goodwill, long hard hours and the dedication of those who worked there. My thoughts were, what idiot invented teambuilding? Must have been a bloke or an American. I wondered what I'd let myself in for and was certain I'd be no good at it. Well, I was just as hot-headed during the sessions in the study as I'd been all those years ago. It was an opportunity to give vent to my anger and frustration and express my feelings, but no one listened anyway. Had anyone explained to me that these sessions were meant to make the team stronger? Did anyone say they were all about identifying our weaknesses so that we could eliminate them and give better service to the customer? No! I'd been thrust in at the deep end and I responded by putting my foot in it and saying the wrong thing.

I found things very difficult because Adrian knew how to wind me up and I'd blow my top at the least provocation. Gradually I realised it wasn't personal. It was all about a particular set of circumstances and the fact that we were not working together as we should have done. So many years of doing things in the same way had left me handcuffed to the past. All these new suggestions were the very opposite of what I'd been taught. Many times I thought of giving up and leaving Highclere Castle as things became tough. But we made a pact during those early days of teambuilding which meant we could air our grievances about various issues and each other, thus developing mutual understanding and improving our working environment.

The following year Adrian decided to upgrade our teambuilding to take in weekends away, so there was more peace and quiet with no telephones ringing and no one having to attend to business. All the managers were taken to London for a weekend of teambuilding to learn to work together and create a better working environment at Highclere. We stayed at the Cumberland Hotel where the managing director of the Forte Group, owners of the hotel, was a great friend of Adrian's. Later we reciprocated by allowing Forte to hold their team-building events at Highclere. Lindsey, who co-ordinated the events at Highclere and had worked there for a number of years, had never experienced teambuilding and neither had I. We were both extremely apprehensive about the days to come.

My first experience as house manager on a teambuilding weekend away was very scary. I worried constantly for weeks prior to the event because I knew I'd be hopeless. It would have been better to tell me I was going the night before. The weekend was a disaster for me as I'd worked myself into such a state that I couldn't sleep. At 4am I went for a walk. I wandered down Oxford Street and found people asleep in cardboard boxes in doorways. It all seemed so unreal; these people weren't tramps but homeless souls with nowhere else to go. As I'd only been to London a couple of times I found it all quite overwhelming.

After a very light-hearted evening session we were given an itinerary for the weekend and I started to relax a little. We had our evening meal at a restaurant, followed by a few drinks afterwards and an early night – well before midnight, anyway. The idea of this teambuilding exercise was to get to know each other better and bond together to create an 'A' Team. Things were very tense during the Saturday session but, after a break for a light lunch, we carried on and one thing really stuck in my mind. We had to decide who (or what?) we'd throw out of a hot air balloon in order to survive. It really surprised me that Lindsey opted to abandon everyone and look after herself – and I was in her team!

The evening involved our 'other halves' coming to London to join us. We dined at Sampans, a restaurant in the Cumberland Hotel. Then we went to see a musical at the theatre. Sunday was very special to me. I visited Covent Garden before going home and it was simply a delight. It has a wonderful atmosphere – all the hustle and bustle and fun of watching the street performers. It was either the food or possibly being novice drinkers which made some of us feel rather fragile at the end of the weekend. I ended up looking forward to next year and hoping Adrian would forget anything that had gone wrong!

After a few sessions the tension surrounding teambuilding eased a little and I realised it could be pleasurable, too. The Oxo Tower restaurant, Chinatown and theatres were great, but I was always on edge during the sessions because of my lack of experience. On another occasion the format changed and we went to the Isle of Wight on a yacht which could accommodate six plus the skipper. Well, this really did it for me because I was scared to death of water and frightened of drowning; it all went back to a mishap when I was young. I was really frightened and did everything I could to get out of it. The first time we set off there was steady rain and it was a question of hanging on for dear life. I was so afraid I sat on the edge of the bed in the cabin all night – or most of it – while Lindsey slept like a baby. We had an excellent meal with lovely wines at a fish restaurant on the island but it still didn't help me sleep. To cap it all, when we left I nipped off to spend a penny and they left me behind! Well, if you could have seen my face it was a picture. On the return journey the Solent was like a millpond but still I hung on to the steering wheel, frightened that something would happen. In the end the engines were turned on to get us back to port – absolute heaven, back home safe at last.

Our last teambuilding exercise was in France but I'd had a new hip put in and went over on the night ferry and back on the hovercraft – even that was bad enough. Some of the others had a rough time crossing the Channel on the yacht and were very seasick. Once we were there I did the driving and it was the first time I'd driven on the wrong side of the road. I took over because Adrian was feeling very fragile and tired from an event he'd attended the night before. We were on our way to Mont St Michel. Through my lack of experience driving on the right I came close to killing everyone as I overtook a lorry then suddenly realised the road was running out. But calmness and determination saved the day and everyone lived to tell the tale.

Over the years, the Carnarvons did not involve themselves with anything designed to encourage team spirit among the Castle staff – they left that to the Castle manager. Just a few words of appreciation now and again, and maybe a get-together at Christmas, would have worked wonders. A bonus, however small, from the Carnarvons at Christmas, given personally to everyone, would have developed strength, loyalty and unity among the staff.

THE LATE 90's AND INTO THE NEW MILLENNIUM – CHANGE

Tony and I had been together for 25 years but agreed our marriage was empty. And so, in 1998/9, we decided to separate. He couldn't come to terms with the fact that I was the breadwinner and kept a roof over our heads. To do this my commitment to Highclere had to be 100 per cent. He worked for Hampshire County Council and had evenings and weekends off, whereas I worked split hours and weekends as well.

When we opened on a commercial basis my world expanded and he couldn't handle that. My new world was full of fun and excitement, so I spent more time at the Castle, meeting people and looking after them. My obsession with Highclere broke the bond between Tony and me, because I was married to the Castle now. Perhaps, if our social life had been different and I had made more of an effort, things might have turned out differently. But not everything was lost because we still had Chris, who was certainly the best thing to have come from our union. Tony still works as a driver for Hampshire County Council, incidentally, and is due to retire in 2006/7.

SIR STANLEY AND LADY CLARKE

In the month of August 2000 a couple we didn't know attended our outdoor concert. They had bid for an auction prize at a charity event comprising a weekend at the Newbury Manor Hotel and a concert at Highclere Castle. Mr and Mrs Stanley Clarke had entered my world, moments before he got his knighthood. I was asked to look after them and they were a wonderful couple, very appreciative. The evening was a success and, to their surprise, they bumped into a couple they knew.

They asked if they could return the next day to look at the gardens and I said it would be my pleasure to accompany them. Stan Clarke talked constantly of his plans for Dunstall Hall, of its history and his dream for the hall and estate. He asked me if I thought that Adrian would consider coming to advise him about conferences and the commercial side of things. I assured him that Adrian had made Highclere very successful and knew everything about conferences, weddings and stately homes. Clearly, Stan was positive Adrian was his man and he was head hunting. What a dream, to form a business from the very beginning!

I hadn't realised who Sir Stanley was. I didn't know he owned numerous racecourses and was in fact a millionaire. To me, he and his wife were a lovely couple, polite, courteous and always smiling. Adrian eventually went to

Dunstall Hall to run the estate and then manage the hall itself. I was asked to go to the hall to give my opinion on what could be done to improve it for business and keep it ticking over until it was refurbished.

If you'd seen Dunstall in the early days, you'd have realised it was destined to be a flourishing business, with a park for people to enjoy the countryside and the magnificent house for entertaining. It was a shame that I'd started a new job which took up my time, so I went in the holidays and on my days off. The doors of the hall and the staircase were in quite a state but, with a lot of tender loving care, they were returned to their original magnificent grandeur.

I knew this was only a temporary arrangement until the whole place was refurbished, but the satisfaction I felt made it all worthwhile. To help out and make sure things were properly organised I was present for Sir Stanley and Lady Clarke's 45th wedding anniversary and for Sir Stanley's 70th birthday party. It was at this second party that I looked after Bob Monkhouse, who had come to entertain the guests. I knew Bob from his visits to Highclere, bless him, and he made some lovely comments in my programme: *"Much love to you, Marvellous Maureen"*, *Bob Monkhouse XXX*. That was such a nice thing to write, although the occasion was spoiled to a degree when I received not a penny piece from Sir Stanley. Adrian had to work hard to get him to dig deep in his pocket for some petrol money.

ADRIAN LEAVES AND A NEW MANAGER ARRIVES

At this point everyone seemed zapped of energy, mainly because of the pressure of functions. The key members of the team had lost their drive, their will to carry on. Adrian was leaving; Lindsey, like me, was going through a divorce and felt unable to commit to anything. Life was a disaster all round and then my collie dog Lady died. On top of that, Chris left to go and live in Blackwater near his new job as a technical consultant for a software company.

Lord and Lady Carnarvon chose Colonel Guy Sayle to take over as Castle manager without any advice or consultation from their family or Adrian. His credentials were endorsed by Lord Carnarvon's friends in the Army and brooked no argument. I remember when they first invited me to Milford Lake House for a drink and a talk about the appointment. I'd been there only a few times and felt uneasy. At least Lord Carnarvon admitted that Guy Sayle knew nothing about running stately homes or a commercial business. 'Great!' I thought. I imagine the only reason they asked me to the House was because Adrian had told them I should be informed of the appointment. I remember asking them if he was a 'hands on' person like Adrian, who would work outside office hours, meet clients and see functions through to the bitter end, even putting tables and chairs back in place in the early hours of the morning if necessary. They assured me that would be no problem! But Lord Carnarvon only stayed for about five minutes before disappearing to make a very important telephone call. Lady Carnarvon was embarrassed but we made polite conversation, mainly about my son Chris.

I soon knew that I would not be able to work with Guy Sayle. On arrival at Highclere, he promptly cancelled appointments made with his new team and went to meet the farm, estate and stud staff first. This did not go down well. He certainly had no interest in my department. As we went around the nursery landing I asked if he was a 'hands on' man who would be present out of office hours. 'Bollocks', he said. Not yet out of the Army, he was already playing the 'big I am' with me. There was also the clear implication that if I did not resign he would sack me, and I was not to mention this conversation to anyone. He was not remotely interested in weddings and functions already booked for the following year. All he appeared to be interested in was learning how to shoot and taking his son out. I knew then that all was lost at Highclere, that with him in charge everything we'd worked for would go down the Swanee. It was quite amazing that Lord Carnarvon could have made such a mistake, placing his trust in a such a creature. And a creature with attitude, to boot.

MY RESIGNATION

Friday, 3rd November 2000. Oh, the sadness and tension I felt. On this day I knew it was time for me to resign after 32 years at Highclere. My heart had not been in the job since Adrian had given his notice in July: I became withdrawn, lacked enthusiasm and felt that all motivation had gone. One of the reasons that I decided to resign and give up something that had meant everything to me for 32 years was the appointment of Guy Sayle as the new manager. Maybe I wasn't thinking straight but I was positive it was time to go and I remained adamant about it. I kept ringing Richard Morris, Lord Carnarvon's managing agent, but got no reply. I sent a fax at 2pm, then left the Castle to drive around the countryside ending up at Stockbridge, a Hampshire village that I was very fond of. The world seemed an emotionless place to me; I had dropped a bombshell and I was waiting for the reaction at Highclere.

Unfortunately Richard Morris wasn't contactable so his office sent the fax straight to Lord Carnarvon. He in turn contacted Colonel Guy Sayle, who instantly telephoned me on my mobile. I remained non-committal regarding my resignation. Anyway, why hadn't Lord Carnarvon called me himself? This wasn't his normal way of doing things. I was hurt, distraught and couldn't bring myself to talk to them.

At the moment I resigned I felt certain that Colonel Guy Sayle was not the right person to take over from Adrian Wiley. I simply had this gut feeling. During the past few years, much had been achieved through sheer hard work with some blood, sweat and tears along the way. Yes, there had been arguments but the business was intact and moving forwards. This was a very sad day. Lady Carnarvon rang on Saturday morning but I couldn't talk to her; indeed, my emotions were running so high that I refused to talk to either Lord or Lady Carnarvon. The only person I could talk to was Richard Morris. Everyone said that Adrian had brainwashed me regarding the Colonel's appointment and that he, Adrian, was put out because he had not been consulted. Over the weekend Lord Carnarvon arrived but things went from bad to worse. In fact, what happened next both hurt and humiliated me, leaving me gutted and extremely angry.

Lord Carnarvon, Guy Sayle and Les Taylor were walking down the corridor to the safe. "Make sure you get the keys off Maureen, Les, and check the safe before she goes because a fragment is missing from an Egyptian artefact". I heard this as I was coming down the stairs from the studio and they were passing the brush room. Lord Carnarvon said that he'd given the fragment to me to take care of and put in the safe. Les told him that the keys were, in fact, always locked in the alarm cupboard. Lord Carnarvon wanted me out of the Castle that evening. Les said if that was what he wanted, he'd have to tell me himself.

Les approached me in the saloon and asked where the fragment was. I said I'd no idea because I'd never seen it. Les told me that Lord Carnarvon had given it to me and I retorted that he definitely hadn't. My honesty and integrity were being challenged, all because I wouldn't talk to Lord Carnarvon over the weekend. I was absolutely furious with him. Here was a man whose family I'd served loyally and faithfully for 32 years questioning my honesty. How could I stay and work for him any longer?

Acting in the proper professional way, Richard Morris came to see me on Monday morning. He, too, asked about the 'fragment' and I reiterated that I hadn't seen it. Apparently it had been hanging in the front hall of Milford Lake House but, as I'd been to Milford just four times in 32 years, I'd never seen it. I was always very precise about where I put things in the safe. Nora, Lord Carnarvon's secretary at Milford Lake House, rang and asked Lindsey to ask me whether I'd seen it, but I simply didn't know what they were on about.

A few weeks later Nora left a message on my answer phone. Lord Carnarvon thought I'd like to know that the 'fragment' had been found. The British Museum had had it all the time! In all my time at Highclere my honesty had never been called into question until then. Sotheby's did an inventory of all the items in the safe soon afterwards. From that moment on, incidentally, no one apart from Colonel Guy Sayle was allowed to remove silver from the safe.

After resigning I said I'd stay until the Buntrocks' shoot on November 7th. The Buntrocks were a very kind American couple who were shareholders in the Harry's racing syndicate. They were lovely people who had offered me a job as housekeeper in America some years before, but I'd refused owing to my circumstances at the time and my love of Highclere. Highclere was my world and my home. Harry and Chica totally agreed with my attitude but would not take a stand against Lord Carnarvon. I was still the loser, but it gave me satisfaction to know that someone could see how I felt. A week later, after a walk, I met Harry in the park. He said I'd let Highclere down, but I was certain it was the other way round. He warned me not to say too much about Colonel Sayle as it wouldn't be in my best interests. I quickly changed the subject and waved cheerio. Harry and Chica knew that my love for Highclere had been lost and could never be regained. But no one knew all the circumstances. They certainly didn't know what Colonel Sayle had said to me whilst walking around the nursery landing. I knew it wouldn't make any difference now, so I held my tongue for a change.

Adrian had asked me to compile a document, detailing all my knowledge and areas of expertise. It was a legacy, if you like, or a guide for the person about to shoulder the burden, someone who was prepared to love Highclere the way I had for 32 years. The documents from all departments were given to Guy Sayle to help him with the running of the Castle. But, instead of using all this information, he simply chose to ignore it.

I told Richard Morris and Lady Carnarvon that the Colonel wasn't the right man for Highclere and their mistake would cost themdearly. Believe me, I said, in six months' time you'll know why I've resigned and see things in a different light. Please tell Lord Carnarvon that I'm sorry but I have to do this to convince you that you've appointed the wrong person. I have to make a stand for what I believe in.

Lady Carnarvon said: "We both made the decision and we think Guy Sayle is the right person for the job". What else could I say? We parted amicably. My decision became irrevocable following the incident of the fragment. I could not forgive the 7th Earl the accusation and I knew I'd never get on with Guy Sayle. Adrian had gone and this man, who hadn't the faintest idea about running anything, had taken over. Guy Sayle told us that when he was in the Army his nickname had been Jonah. Need I say more?

Following my letter of resignation there was a reply from Richard Morris on the 7th November summarising the termination details of my employment. Apparently my first letter hadn't been received and they didn't know I had a doctor's certificate. I was stressed out but didn't realize it. I hadn't had a day off for such a long time, which was mainly my own fault, but no one could take over and we were so busy. I couldn't let go, really. I can see that now and I realise the strain had caught up with me. The postscript at the bottom of Richard's letter showed that he hadn't heard about Lord Carnarvon's apparent distrust of me where the safe was concerned. He was unaware of Lord Carnarvon's vindictiveness towards me and just assumed, I suppose, that I'd got on my high horse again. But it wasn't like that at all. I was very hurt and angry and no longer wished to be at the Castle.

I was still hurting when Lady Carnarvon and I talked. But subsequent discussions with Richard Morris worked in my favour to a degree because the subject of royal trainer Dick Hern's recently republished book, in which he mentioned his dismissal, cropped up, while the reminder about the doctor's certificate and length of time I'd been at Highclere also helped. I did not know the late Major Hern, but everyone in racing said he was a superb trainer and totally loyal to the Carnarvons, yet they'd wanted him out within a month! Lord Carnarvon gave me extra time to stay in the house. With any luck I'd find another position before the end of January 2001 as they knew I couldn't get any work before Christmas on a permanent basis. After further talks with Richard Morris he said he'd have a word with Lord Carnarvon about severance pay but I'd have to wait until I left. I'm still waiting. It seems that Richard did indeed ask the 7th Earl but he refused to pay me anything. That's what you get for 32 years of loyalty, dedication and love for Highclere.

WAITING TO LEAVE HIGHCLERE

The spark went out of my life when I resigned and knew that my days at Highclere were numbered. I had no motivation, no goals to achieve. What was I to do? At some point I'd have to summon up the will and energy to go back to work, but what then? My world was in limbo, my mind not focused on what I should be doing. I needed to be looking after people, using my knowledge and expertise. There are not many jobs that require skills like these. My knowledge was all about the way they did things once upon a time! Everything today, especially the day-to-day running of a business, seems to be about computers and hi-technology. I had not had that experience and did not know where to start.

It's pretty obvious where my strengths lie. I make people feel welcome and at home. At Highclere I always put clients first, regardless of how I felt myself. That was the way I went about things, with a big smile at the door and a willingness to help with anything. A computer can indicate what a client requires, but his personal needs can only be taken care of by a person, someone like you or me. People are not machines. Can a computer clean and maintain silver? Can it act quickly in a domestic crisis? I had lost my way and needed help. Leaving Highclere was like having a broken heart after a love affair – a love affair lasting 32 years!

Life goes on, of course. I had resigned and would spend only a few more weeks at the Castle. I was really down, but sometimes things come along at the right time and it just so happened that I had the chance to go on a small partridge shoot a matter of days later. I felt excited, which showed I still had the spirit to fight back and enjoy life. But it would take time.

MY FIRST DAY ON A SMALL PARTRIDGE SHOOT AFTER 32 YEARS AT HIGHCLERE – 8th NOVEMBER 2000

Getting up at 6am didn't deter me, although I thought the cold might, but it turned out to be a great day. We arrived at Jack Rolfe's (a shooting buddy of Adrian Wiley's) for a huge breakfast cooked by Sue, his other half. 1996 home-made sloe gin rounded off the meal and Adrian, Jack and Bill Porritt ended with oval, soft-centred dark chocolates, which were served by Sue afterwards. Unfortunately, Sue couldn't come. They had drainage problems in their garden and she was holding the fort for Jack. A kitty was formed at £5 per head for the total of birds shot – even Sue went in.

We arrived at the pub for the start of the shoot, booted up and then set out for the shooting ground. The medicine trolley came out and there was again sloe gin as the beaters got everything organised. Pegs had been drawn and we were put into position. Pegs, or stands where you shoot from, are drawn at the beginning of a shoot and then, on each drive, you move up 2 pegs or even 3 to the next stand. The head person gives a short talk before the shoot to explain this and adds: 'No ground game, no low birds, and please don't shoot the beaters!' Until this drive I hadn't really understood this, but suddenly everything fell into place.

The beaters drove the partridge over. I hadn't realized how a shoot ran until now. I soon learned how to be a loader. Wow! What an experience. It was a dry day but the wind cut through my fingertips. I was promptly advised to tuck my blue-tinted digits into my jacket side pockets. The medicine trolley came out again after the first drive; this really is what it's all about. The position of the next drive was around the valley, so we walked. After each drive the dogs showed their skill at picking up. The springers and labradors scamper around the bushes searching for the shot game, then proudly bring them to their handlers. After the odd battle with the dogs for possession of the birds, they are brought to the game wagon where they're sorted, tied into braces and hung over a rail until the end of the shoot and the final game count.

We drove to another drive that was based on the hills. We were peg 8 for this drive. The beaters were above us on the hills, beating the partridge up. They could easily have been shot. My 'Eh, oop!' when a bird came over caused a few laughs; apparently you just say 'over', when a bird flies over. Being on peg 8 we didn't get any. Lucky Jack, as he's called, was getting all the birds. It didn't matter where he was or which peg he was on, the birds always flew in his direction. The whistle blew for the end of the drive.

We drove to our next drive, but the opposite way. Out came the medicine trolley again, to keep out the cold – or so I was told. Lucky Jack, in his favoured position again, was in top form. Consequently we didn't have many birds at all, but it was fun and absolutely great. The end of the shoot drew to a close as a few partridge were needed for Saturday's shoot. As the partridge were put into braces the number slowly crept up to what I'd suggested – 151. The last picker-up walked slowly down the hill with his arms full and Lucky Jack produced 2 partridge from his coat pockets. Sue was closest to the final tally of 163 so she'd won the kitty. I was given it in case they spent it at the pub or lost it playing 'shut the box'.

Then it was back to the pub for a few jars, though not for me as I was driving, and a roast lunch comprising roast beef, Yorkshire pudding and vegetables with cheese and coffee to follow. Mind you, someone could have told them how to cook the Yorkshire and the roast potatoes! Many games of 'shut the box' followed, and many pints of Guinness. The landlady was getting very impatient as she wanted to have her own lunch and put her feet up. Finally we decided to leave, but only after Bill Porritt had managed to obtain 20 brace of partridge for £10 – what a man.

Arriving back at Jack's, Sue had supper waiting. After a few laughs and many tales we could see Sue was furious with Jack. We thought it was because we'd stopped on the way back to see Tim's dad, a friend of Jack's. He was indeed a character and very grateful that we'd stopped by – it really made his day. However, this was not the problem. Jack's office staff had upset Sue; she made no bones about it and it nearly blew up into a full-scale row. Lucky Jack defused the situation fairly rapidly. More drinks were downed and cider was the topic of conversation. Adrian and Sue were now betting on who would drink a pint of dry cider that Sue had brought. Adrian took the bet for a laugh, managed to win and his expression was something to behold.

Sue was over the moon at having won the kitty and that also calmed her down. As the evening drew to a close we all made a move to go home, as Bill Porritt plus all his partridge had to be delivered safely. It was a wonder that Jack's dog hadn't eaten them all. Adrian's new Land Rover Discovery was a total disaster, covered in mud both inside and out. It would take him days to recover and get around to cleaning it! Sandy McCabe (Bill's partner) was awaiting him on his return and we stayed for a while before continuing on to Highclere. I was dropped off totally exhausted, full of memories and having enjoyed a wonderful day. My first day's partridge shooting was a great experience and I loved every minute of it – I'd even been praised for being a good stuffer, which made my day, especially as I'd started out not even knowing what a loader did.

I slept soundly that night, deeply satisfied with the way my day had gone. You have to get rid of the hurt somehow, and I had made a good start.

MY FIRST PHEASANT SHOOT – HOST MARCO PIERRE WHITE

I think Adrian was determined to cheer me up and there was time for one more special occasion – my very first pheasant shoot, hosted by Marco Pierre White. My God, what a long day! Up at 6am and after a bacon and egg bap we left at 7.15 to get to Petworth for 9.15, where we stopped in the market square to find coffee. No such luck – only the bakery with a take-away drinks service. It's such a beautiful town but no one seems to open before 9.30 except the bakery. We carried on to Petworth Golf Club where, at one of the cottages, we were welcomed with coffee/orange juice and the chance to spend a penny.

Booting up, we set off for the first drive. Before we left, Marco greeted me very warmly and said a quick hello to Adrian, as well. I thought he seemed a bit distant towards him but perhaps it was too early in the morning for anyone to exchange anything other than brief pleasantries. As we approached the first drive and saw this huge ploughed field I thought: 'Oh no, he's (the shoot captain) not expecting us to walk over that!' He was, but luckily we didn't get that stand and had the woods, as did Marco, which was a blessing. When we had actual pegs we were either last or first, but believe me neither was any good. A few birds came over. Adrian, for whom I was loading, was approached at the end of the drive by the lady who was picking up. She asked him if he could take the pheasants she'd picked up back to the game wagon. Laden with pheasants we walked back to the 4 x 4's. After a brief session we continued to the next drive.

Unfortunately we were put into a low-key position. A few birds drifted over but the shooting was no good at all for Adrian. Earlier on we'd discovered we were shooting right through to late afternoon before having lunch. Dear me, we were starving; someone might have told us before. We only had a few sweets – four Topics – and two flasks of mulled wine between us. Dear oh dear. We offered Marco a Topic. "Oh, I'll only have half", he said. But as we followed him I noticed that he polished it off. Mind you, he was a huge fellow, the kind of person you want to hug and mother, especially with his curly hair and wonderful smile.

I know this was only a two hundred-bird day but the betting on the day's shoot was way over the top. The birds seemed to fly over in all directions and we had very little success. Shooting seemed to be all about waiting for the birds to come over, drinking coffee, getting stuck into the medicine trolley or freezing.

The next drive would be followed by another, then on to the golf links and hopefully the chance to pay a visit – but no such luck! Walking or dragging our boots through mud and yet another ploughed field, we stood at our pegs and then the rain came down. I wondered what the hell I was doing there.

But then the pheasants started to fly. Wow, what high birds! Then I understood what the art of shooting was all about. Proficiency came with a great deal of practice and I needed more tuition in loading to react faster, also remembering to keep the bag closed in case it rained. Amazing! Didn't think of that one, which showed what a complete novice I was. Dripping wet, we hauled ourselves back over the ploughed field to the 4 x 4's. On one of the drives we saw a roe deer hurrying out of the woods. For once he wasn't the quarry and he seemed to understand. We thought we'd go on the duck drive next but apparently everyone had decided that enough was enough and we went back to the cottage for a late lunch. We did see a covey of partridges but never actually shot any. As we were all desperate for the facilities, speed was of the essence!

Lunch smelt wonderful. The table where we'd had coffee first thing had been pulled out to cater for 12, the fire was blazing and everything looked very inviting. Then suddenly I saw something move in the fireplace. I was reassured that the grey parrot knew what he was doing and that he'd move if he became too hot! There were drinks before lunch. Marco sat himself down, quite at home, and everyone else did too. It just seemed the most natural thing to do. Twenty minutes later we were called into lunch. Owing to the fact that the duck drive had been cancelled we had no potatoes because we'd arrived earlier than expected. Hot vegetable soup, steak and kidney pudding, vegetables, three choices of pudding, cheese and biscuits and then coffee. I watched Marco's face for his reaction to the food and it quite astonished me to see that he was tucking into the meal with great gusto but refused the sweet. He loved the ginger beer as he didn't drink alcohol. One of Marco's friends won the sweepstake, his uncle from Italy nearly won it and the atmosphere was very relaxed.

Everyone had enjoyed a fun day. It was really great, especially when Marco said how sad he was that Adrian and I had left Highclere. The only reason he'd booked the shoots at Highclere was because we were there. He was so relaxed, smoked a lot and was excellent company. Shooting dominated his spare time. Out of 28 days he shot on about 22 of them. His companions were made up of chefs, business people and friends – what a lovely combination. He was the same with everyone, and everyone wanted to be there. On our departure he hugged me and thanked me for coming. I said that I was delighted and he'd certainly made my first day of pheasant shooting a wonderful experience. Adrian was tipping the keeper as this is what Guns do after a shoot. They paid him for his day based on the number of birds shot, which was just over 200. Not bad when you think that we hadn't shot many ourselves.

Every shoot is different on every estate, depending on weather conditions and how the keepers look after the birds. The shooting at Highclere – the standard of the birds and the way they're brought over the drives – has always been the best. 32 years and I hadn't realised what shoots were about. Up until now I'd only been involved with looking after Guns and guests pre-shoot and at the end of the day. I'd thought this shooting lark was extremely overrated but, at the end of the day, I found it absolutely wonderful. Lots of walking, fresh air, mud, then rain followed by good food. How exhilarating the actual shoot was, beyond anything I can explain. You have to be there, soak up the atmosphere and see for yourself. One day, I promised myself, I'll be on a shoot at Highclere and experience the best and see what I've missed. Unfortunately, it never quite happened.

TIME TO MOVE ON – FEBRUARY 2001

But when I got back to the house it was cold and empty, a bit like me. I had lost faith in everything and it was time to move on. You acquire a good many things over 32½ years and they all had to be cleared out. After weeks of packing I lost the energy and desire to do that, as well. One whole bedroom became an Aladdin's Cave of objects which I gave to whomever wanted them – mainly the church and the hospital. Janet Benney, a good friend, stored my furniture and even offered me a home if I was really desperate. For me, this was hardly a propitious start to the new century, although I was more fortunate than others, or so my friend Lindsey kept telling me. The following June, 2001 I eventually went to see my doctor who told me I had severe depression and should have come to see him in November 2000 when I handed in my notice instead of trying to handle it myself.

Guy Sayle and I tolerated each other until my departure on the 5th February 2001. Within ten months he single-handedly destroyed what everyone had built up and believed in. Apparently, he told people who came to the Castle for recces that I'd been sacked. He'd got rid of me because I wouldn't co-operate with him. I chanced upon the fact that he was being paid £10,000 more than Adrian, he had a new car and alterations were made to Adrian's old house to accommodate his family. Why hadn't they appreciated Adrian and done these things for him? But I had no regrets and I left with my head held high.

Leaving the Castle was traumatic for all of us and made a mark on everyone's lives. Lindsey left Highclere after two months of Guy Sayle's regime. She, too, had suffered a bad bout of depression and moved to Hungerford for a while, having separated from Martin. Her depression and the state of her personal life led her to try to commit suicide, which had a drastic effect on me, as well. She didn't know what she was taking but ended up in hospital, which proved to be a turning point in her life. It had all come about through events at Highclere. Afterwards she came to stay with me at Marlow to recuperate. After receiving my support through her depression and a very messy divorce, she left after 3 years on 6 April 2004 to return to Newbury, where I hope she will be able to enjoy a normal, happy life.

Looking back on life at Highclere

Going back over my time at Highclere I can see now that, had someone guided me from the early stages, I should not have been so possessive and protective of my position. I know now how Robert Taylor felt when the caterers Sarah and Mary arrived – it was like history repeating itself. Robert's upbringing and strictness made a deep impression upon me. I couldn't let go of anything. Many times I feared that if I were to share the knowledge I had in my head, everything I'd worked for at the place I loved would be lost. I was infatuated with Highclere and protective of everything there, but this had the effect of shutting me out as barriers went up. It also turned me into someone I was not. I was suddenly this high and mighty person who was in control and woe betide anyone who forgot it. I was a bitch quite a lot of the time, mainly because of the pressure of being put in charge and the worry of having it all taken away. My life at Highclere was like a yo-yo. One minute I was meeting and greeting and the next I was pushed into the background. No wonder I was spiteful, bossy and protective.

Sometimes I did two people's jobs, working extremely long hours and not really eating. I also drank quite a lot of alcohol during my evenings at home which made me extremely relaxed but also made me very irritable the next day. Many times I was inadequate but stumbled along hoping for the best, not realising that other people felt the same. I couldn't communicate and express myself to anyone and no one understood how I felt about Highclere. My trouble was that I couldn't relax. I'd fought so hard to achieve something and try to make my parents, especially my mother, proud of me. Nothing else mattered. She once told me it was my twin brother Malcolm she loved, not me, even when I gave her a photograph of The Queen, Queen Mother and myself taken at Highclere. She showed no emotion, there was no praise and another barrier went up.

I realise that no one is perfect, but I was taught perfection, precision and to have very high standards and I couldn't understand why other people fell short. Robert would have turned in his grave to see the careless attitude of some of the people employed at Highclere and he would have laughed, too, to think that the person with whom he battled constantly, the cheeky upstart who invaded his territory in September 1968, had achieved his goal of maintaining high standards at Highclere. In many ways I have much to thank him for. For many years he was so strict that I couldn't call anyone by their Christian name. It was considered very familiar and, being old fashioned, I called everyone in domestic service by their title. Everyone was relaxed about Christian names except me. Robert taught me the basics when I learned to appreciate fine wines, how to clean the silver properly, lay a table in great detail by measuring place settings and the distances between chairs, indeed the fundamentals of butlering without actually being a butler. I was very eager to learn and hadn't quite grasped the nature of the gift he'd already bestowed upon me. Funnily enough, when the first caterers, Sarah and Mary, took over at Highclere in 1988, I became his ally, not something I'd expected but then again I was from the 6th Earl's era and he didn't really have anyone else.

There are many places in Highclere where you can observe people and hear what they are saying, and I knew all of them! They say you don't hear good things by listening in to other people's conversations and sometimes this is true. Sometimes I think back to the times when I sat on the staircase sobbing and then had to be very still because I heard someone coming. Then hearing my name mentioned – people were talking about me! Now I realise why. I must have been a right old dragon to have put them through what I did, especially Ann Collins and Mandy Marfleet. Mandy and I both wanted something but in different ways. I had a job to do, and Mandy wanted that job. She itched to acquire my knowledge, but I felt she wasn't the right person to use it. Conversations between Adrian Wiley and Dorothy Channing-Williams, who was banqueting manager at the time, sometimes amazed me. On one occasion Adrian was telling her to get rid of my son if he was useless. Fair enough, he had a lot to learn, but he was not useless. Chris had an attitude problem but he was a hard worker. He lasted 4 years out of the five that Adrian was at Highclere. It was during the reign of the Marfleets that Chris finally left.

It's odd, looking back now and wondering what would have happened if I'd passed on my knowledge sooner. Would I have left Highclere before I did? Now I know that I was stressed and depressed. Many times I could have left but it didn't seem right somehow. Adrian Wiley and I crossed swords on many occasions about passing on my expertise. My attitude was, why should I? If they knew their job why did they need my input?

Life after Highclere

After the emotional departure from my home of 32 years, I took up residence in Marlow as cook/housekeeper to Sir Harry and Lady Djanogly. I have been with them now for over 4 years. It took me a while to settle into my new life, which I found lonely after all the hustle and bustle of Highclere. Gone are the days when icicles hung inside my bedroom window and Tony's false teeth froze on the bathroom windowsill through lack of heating. I now live in a cottage with central heating, something that I hadn't had for 30 years. I am part of a family which appreciates my knowledge and has given me back my self-esteem and dignity. I am custodian of their house and collection. When their family and grandchildren arrive they greet me as part of their family. Their rebellious border terrier Dusky gave me hell for the first couple of years but has come to love me. We respect each other and are constant companions. Of course there are other differences between life now and at Highclere, notably with regard to the gardens. They have four gardeners twice a week. James Firth is the head gardener and the garden is perfect – not like at Highclere, where inconsistent standards invariably prompted analysis and debate. Why was it that standards within the Castle were so high, but as soon as you stepped outside the gardeners appeared to be in a totally different, relaxed world where you were relieved to find anything being done at all? On a personal level I had to put up with the unwelcome advances of Philip, one of the gardeners' assistants, but more generally there was no discipline, no adherence to the work ethic. On one occasion Adrian Wiley even had to get his own mower and mow the croquet lawn when they refused to mow it for an important event at the weekend.

I did go back to Highclere. The July following my resignation I was travelling south and decided to go to Highclere Castle to find out about the new dining refurbishment. The guides and Colin gave me such a reception it brought a great lump to my throat. I walked around Highclere at my leisure and it nearly broke my heart to see the devastation. There were no red runners to protect the beautiful carpets, the floors were filthy and the sheen had disappeared. The furniture had been scratched, watermarked and hardly polished. The fireplaces were dirty and full of dust. Light bulbs all over the place needed replacing. There were giant cobwebs, especially on the staircase. Gaffa tape had been taped to the main stateroom floors and taken off the polish that remained. The front door was peeling and had not been washed for months and there was green algae on the slabs outside.

At the bottom of the stairs a sheet of paper telling you which way to go was stuck to the pillars with blutac. People were crossing over outside the boudoir to get downstairs to the Egyptian Room. Doors and windows were open, even on guided tours. The office which had been mine was full of plates, broken chairs, toilet rolls and cleaning products and the door was wide open. Carpets were dirty and askew, especially in the drawing room. The back corridor looked like it did when I first arrived thirty-two years before – a total mess. The servery stairs were chipped where people had bumped tables down rather than carry them. The servery itself had a lovely layout but the floor was filthy for a kitchen and all the worktops were dirty. What a shambles, but why should I worry?

I hadn't taken into account the emotional turmoil involved in returning to Highclere. What possessed me to go back I don't know, it was as if I had to lay some ghosts to rest before I could move on in life. I was truly mortified to see what Guy Sayle had done. I hadn't prepared myself for the inevitable changes; a place I had devoted my life to had gone downhill so rapidly. How appalling it was. Obviously no one cared any more, inside or out. I wasn't being vindictive. I felt sorry for Highclere, its reputation and the family. Most of all, though, I felt for Diana, who needed more help and whose hard work and unstinting efforts could not withstand a tidal wave of indifference. I later heard from friends that the 7th Earl, returning from Wyoming, gave Guy Sayle his notice in August, 2001. He was to be off the estate by September 21st. What a surprise!

It was on this visit that I discovered that the painting of the Countess of Pembroke, Margaret Sawyer, had been moved. In 1685 Sir Godfrey Kneller was commissioned by Sir Robert Sawyer to paint his daughter, who was the 8th Countess of Pembroke. She died in 1706 leaving Highclere to her second son, Robert Sawyer Herbert. There is an old family legend that records that if this portrait is ever moved, DISASTER will strike the Herberts. This portrait that hangs to the left of the fireplace in the State Dining Room was moved on the orders of Colonel Guy Sayle, and as 'Jonah' had driven off all the committed, knowledgeable, caring staff who were aware of the curse, there was no one there to protect the family from the disaster that followed – which was, sadly, the passing of the 7th Earl, who died prematurely from a massive heart attack. Of course, you may put it all down to coincidence. But, after reading this book, can anyone really be sure?

CONCLUSION

Adrian Wiley is now back at Highclere. Sir Stanley Clarke died of cancer after a long, brave battle and Adrian left Dunstall Hall after three years because the 8th Earl urgently needed him back. Highclere Castle had rapidly sunk into the red again.

Six generations of the Carnarvon family have been privileged to act as custodians of Highclere, and each has tried to maintain the Castle according to the wishes, or the dream if you like, of their illustrious ancestor. What would the 3rd Earl of Carnarvon, the man who created this splendid home, think about the changes that have occurred down through the ages? Would he have been mortified if suddenly able to see into the future? To see the Castle tower rooms neglected, with holes in the ceiling and lack of maintenance allowing the rain to seep through? To see some of the glorious trees uprooted to make way for tennis courts? The Carnarvons neither sought nor valued your opinion, yet it would have been very difficult, had I still worked at Highclere, to have stood by and said nothing when the Yew Tree evergreen oaks and box that had been so cleverly planted by the 3rd Earl to shield his new Castle from the Georgian aspect were well and truly axed. Not only that, but their replacement was a humble beech hedge that loses its foliage every year and makes the arrival of winter only too obvious. Will the new generation of Carnarvons put back into the Castle what they have taken out? That remains to be seen, although it is most unlikely to turn out the way its creator intended.

As a housekeeper, I was always having to deal with the unexpected and remain silent. But, given my time again, I would still have gone to Highclere. The Castle will always be special to me and the memories cannot be erased. I imagine many people will be envious of my experiences, and all I can say is that I was lucky and privileged to have had them. I once said to Sheila Crook (former manageress of the Castle Gift Shop): "Highclere has this mystical hold over everyone; when it has you in its grasp it never lets go".

Adrian showing off the Wyverns

Chris helping to lay the table for a formal meal

Adrian pouring the 1962 Petrus at his 50th birthday party

Wines from Adrian's 50th birthday party including the 1962 Petrus

Maureen at Ascot, not watching the horses

Maureen with HM The Queen and Queen Mother, 1996

Gerald Benney by Paul Benney

Paul Hodges

Lindsay Giles
by Paul Hodges

Maureen with her younger
brother, David, and nephew
Gavin, after the Raff Concert

Hon. Harry Herbert inspecting the cricket pitch

Spring-cleaning at Highclere

Spring-cleaning was not always done in the spring in the latter years as we were always too busy, so we fitted it in when we had time. Before the really busy times we had nearly three weeks to a month to spring-clean so each room had a good turn out. This presented a problem when we were open 7 days a week, plus weddings or functions in the summer, conferences and spring weddings, shoots and other events throughout the rest of the year.

Chimneys were cleaned before spring-cleaning took place as they always made such a mess. Furniture had to be covered, carpets rolled back and lampshades removed. A mini scaffold tower was loaned to us by Withers the decorators and work started. Walls and paintwork were washed, curtains and drapes hoovered. Stonework around the saloon was hoovered and shields washed and polished – this used to take 3-4 days to complete. Floors were stripped of polish and re-polished. Upholstery was hoovered, leather washed with vinegar and water and leather cream applied. I even stripped, sandpapered and polished the shutters in the boudoir and smoking rooms.

The chandelier in the drawing room was cleaned once a year. This was a major project taking each piece off, hand washing, drying and polishing with a linen cloth. The mini tower came in handy then. Up I went with my cleaning materials, a flask of tea and a stereo Walkman – moments of bliss in a world of my own.

Fireplaces used to take up to half a day just to clean one, using black lead and brushes, then sanding and oiling the steel. A good hot bath was essential as the dust went everywhere on your skin. The only person who came up to my standard when it came to cleaning the fireplaces was Richard. Leather panelling in the saloon was cleaned and creamed once a year, usually on a Good Friday when no one else was working. One year, I was shocked to see that someone had drawn moustaches with crayon on a few of the leather faces. Maybe it happened after a wedding, and I mentioned it to the Castle manager. He was horrified until he discovered that every face was the same! What a complete wally I felt. I'd been so engrossed in cleaning the leather, which hadn't really been cleaned before, that I hadn't noticed. This was quite a good story for him to tell visitors when he showed them round!

Furniture, bookshelves, fixtures and fittings had to be treated for woodworm and kept monitored for activity. Carpets were repaired and cleaned where necessary but the larger State Room carpets were specialist cleaned and were away sometimes for six weeks or more. Blind and pull strings were cleaned and repaired. Lampshades were regularly dusted but during spring-cleaning time repairs were done. Woodwork in the saloon and staircase was re-polished but this took at least six weeks, because in some places the mini tower was needed. Gold leaf was inspected and noted for repair. Silks were gently brushed where necessary. Fabrics were maintained by Prue Lane-Fox. The paintings were left to the experts but the frames were gently cleaned.

Hoovers and polishers had their yearly overhaul even though maintained throughout the year. Bedrooms were not the top priority but drawers and wardrobes were dusted out, bedspreads and curtains cleaned and paintwork washed where necessary. Baths and sinks were thoroughly cleaned during general cleaning so this wasn't of major importance during spring-cleaning. Tapestries and marble statues were only dusted during the year as specialist cleaning was needed if any major repairs were done. Concrete stairs were hand-scrubbed. Clocks were maintained on a regular basis by Mr May in Newbury. If any repairs were necessary to the furniture or major woodworm treatment needed, we called on Stan Bosley, antique restorer to the 6th and 7th Earls of Carnarvon.

Paintwork was a constant problem and Pat and Mike Withers always took on any work when repairs were needed because it was important to have trustworthy people in the house. China had to be delicately washed and dried to prevent breakage.

Mirrors were cleaned monthly so it wasn't appropriate to have anything major done to them.

The saloon and the landings were constantly beset by cobwebs. Below, stonework was done with the extended fluffy on a regular basis, so it wasn't a problem. The spring and summer sun always caused us headaches as it shone through the saloon and cobwebs were more visible, thus giving us more work.

In the Library there were over 2,000 books and the shelves and books all had to be cleaned. This was an ongoing operation and was left alone during spring-cleaning as it was done a section at a time.

Before major functions took place, the front doors were sanded down and re-varnished and the outside lights washed and cleaned. Concrete on the door-step and other slabs were scrubbed manually. Outside window maintenance by Rainracer was put into place and the rest of the windows cleaned.

Provision for cleaning any carpets in the tea rooms, studio or major rooms was made by Malcolm Clarke, who would always come overwhen required. His firm also cleaned the windows as he and his brother started their window-cleaning business in 1967 at the Castle and always loved to come back to Highclere. Malcolm had many happy memories of the place, having met his first wife there when she helped Mrs Reid.

The old nurseries were briefly spring-cleaned but the most important rooms were the ones in use, so sometimes the others were left. At some point the tower had to be spring-cleaned and flies disposed of, so again this was done when time permitted. When I first arrived at Highclere Mrs Reid was housekeeper and my first job when I moved over to her department in 1987 was to clear the tower of flies. This meant shovelling into a black bin bag all the flies, which were a few inches thick in all the rooms. It was a disgusting job and I swore it wouldn't get into the same state again. The flies were a great headache as they always bred in the stonework. When the spring sun arrived, they had a field day.

Christmases at Highclere

Christmases at Highclere meant more work for everyone, especially when Lady Penelope, the 6th Earls' daughter, her husband Gerrit van der Woude and their three children arrived. It was a family gathering and everyone came for Christmas Day. Everyone would join in the celebrations, which started on Christmas Eve with the choir from Highclere Church singing carols and the hand bells joining them. There was an enormous 14-foot Christmas tree and a roaring log fire in the saloon. Mince pies and mulled wine were passed around. The family would have an 8pm dinner and after that we were allowed home at about 10pm. It was a 6am start for some of us but Lord Carnarvon and the family would go to church for the midnight service.

On Christmas Day a huge breakfast for the family would be prepared from York ham, kidneys etc. Lunch would always be very traditional fare, with drinks beforehand. The turkey was prepared for the oven on Christmas Eve and put into a very large copper container. The kitchen range had to be stoked up before anything could be cooked. I hated this job and emptying ashes – and I still do! The staff had their lunch when everyone had finished upstairs, which didn't give us much time. Misson went home to have lunch with his wife and two sons and then came back in the evening so that Robert could have time with his family. Afternoon tea would be left for the Earl and his family and then I always came back to do a light dinner for them, which was at 8pm. The family would stay for the traditional Boxing Day shoot.

This pattern continued for a few years until the 6th Earl grew older and was unable to cope. He would sometimes go to Milford Lake House which is where Lord Porchester, later the 7th Earl, lived or spend a quiet day in his study. It was always a tradition for the 6th Earl to give a present to his staff of two weeks' wages, which we went to his study to receive on Christmas Day.

I remember Christmas 1977 in particular because it was nearly a disaster. The whole Carnarvon family were coming to lunch and the morning started like any Christmas morning, up early and at work by 6am to stoke up the coal range to get the temperature up. The huge turkey was put into a copper dish about 3ft long. The wind played an important role in getting the stove going as it helped to draw the fire in the range. If absolutely necessary we had a Calor gas cooker as a stand-by but on this occasion the dish was too large for the oven.

Ivy, the then cook, and I carried on preparing the meal as usual, but then we had the most devastating news: Ivy's husband Lewis (nicknamed Polly), already very ill, had taken a turn for the worse. She'd left him in bed because of her early start. I called Robert Taylor and made him aware of the situation as Ivy was taken home. At that time we had very few staff which we saw as quite a blessing in a way because we were going to have our staff lunch in the old housekeeper's room (now the tea room). The turkey was temporarily forgotten and everything came to a standstill. As the morning went on no one had noticed the direction of the wind and the oven had failed to rise to the required temperature. Quick action was needed as lunch time was drawing near: There was no alternative but to fry and grill the turkey, so that is how we set about making lunch for the Carnarvons. It was a sad day for Ivy (like every Christmas after that) because her husband died during the Queen's Speech. I never had any comments from the family about the lunch – no doubt Robert had told them the news and they'd made allowances.

When the 6th Earl died and we opened for corporate business we always closed on Christmas Day so that the family could have the day to themselves. The tree was still between 12 and 14 feet high and always to the right of the fireplace. It was great to keep some traditions going but they only wanted a quiet Christmas and so there was no traditional Christmas Eve, no choir, no mince pies or mulled wine – nothing but the Christmas tree with a roaring log fire. The 7th Earl and all the family would have their lunch, again traditional fare, then watch The Queen's speech on a specially-installed television set before everyone had presents and went home. Quite often on Boxing Day the shoot took place from Milford Lake House so the Castle would be free for a special tour – generally from the Hilton Hotel.

On three occasions I cooked Christmas lunch for the Carnarvon family, even when we had chefs. One chef's (Chris Andrews') father was very poorly and he said that he couldn't do the lunch as he was going to Lancashire to see his parents. Chica really hauled him over the coals for this, but his father died and he knew he'd made the right decision. He left shortly afterwards.

My son Chris and I did the lunch between us one year as no one could suggest an alternative. Another chef, Mark Greenfield, had a young family so I offered to do lunch for him and he was very grateful. I realised too late that Christmas should be spent at home with your own family. But the Carnarvons were very grateful and I did get a personal thank-you and a lovely letter from Lady Carnarvon.

THE CHRISTMAS TREE

The Christmas tree usually came in during the first week in December and I had the job of decorating it. It was generally brought in the day before as it took most of the day to complete. For many years it was placed near the 3rd Countess's portrait to the right of the fireplace. Commercial functions dented tradition and it came to be placed under the 3rd Earl's portrait. It was beautifully positioned and you could see it from everywhere. There were traditional decorations, five sets of fairy lights and sometimes a wooden fairy on the top which had been made by one of the guides.

One year, Greg Rusedski's wedding was due to take place just before Christmas, they asked permission to have someone decorate the tree for them. It was a lovely idea and turned out to be very modern. Lady Carnarvon loved it. It was a great relief to know that everyone liked it modern and not traditional, because that saved me a lot of time and energy! Quite often the tree was in place for six weeks. It was so magnificent one year that Adrian Wiley decided it would be the Christmas card twelve months on. Like everyone else after the joy of Christmas and New Year, we had the major task of taking the tree down. This took just as long as putting it up and created an awful mess. But it was great to see everyone enjoying themselves drinking mulled wine and warming themselves before roaring log fires. Just breathing in the atmosphere was exhilarating.

I'll always remember one occasion when the tree was positioned under the portrait of the 3rd Countess. The wedges hadn't been put into the base properly and, as I went to turn the lights off at the end of the day, the tree started to fall. Goodness, didn't I panic! I grabbed hold of the tree and still it moved. It was a two-handed job. Can you imagine it? I stretched my foot to reach the phone but in vain. I shouted for help but no one heard. I had great confidence that something or someone would rescue me and after an hour I was greatly relieved to see my son Chris coming to see why I hadn't come home. He said I should have let the tree fall – could you see me doing that after a whole day's work? No way!

One year Stan Anstie collected the tree and, right out of the blue, said: "Maureen, life is like a Christmas tree, you get to the top and then you either fall or slip down." I could never understand what he meant. I've had a good life so I must still be going up the tree. Bless him.

Ghost stories

THE CHILD IN THE TREE

Outside the kitchens a tree near the old church ruins was surrounded by brickwork. The cement was badly cracked. The legend goes that a child was sealed in the tree for 100 years. The child was wicked and used to taunt people during her life. She was sealed in the tree and bricked up so she wouldn't do any more nasty things. One day Misson the chauffeur told the 6th Earl that he'd just seen the child's ghost; he was in a terrible state. Misson was Irish but definitely a teetotaller. He was so scared that the 6th Earl had the brickwork re-sealed, just to reassure Misson that no ghost would approach him.

One day, a few years later Ivy, who always came to work at 8.30am on the dot, had not arrived. I made the 6th Earl's breakfast and became a bit worried. Going to the back door of the kitchen I saw a very large tree which had crashed on to the drive where Ivy's car was always parked. Later Ivy arrived -and was she surprised! The legend went that the tree would fall down after 100 years and the child's spirit would be released. There was no wind or anything unusual that day so no one had an explanation. You can still see the remains of the tree and brickwork on the kitchen side of the Castle (the Georgian entrance). No one has seen the ghost since and no presence was felt when mediums came to the Castle to contact spirits of the dead.

LADIES IN BLACK

Ivy went to see the 6th Earl one day to agree the menus and a lady in a dark cloak went down the corridor so she said "Good morning", not thinking any more about it until she passed Robert's office opposite the tea rooms. "Who was that, Robert?" Ivy asked. Robert said: "I've not seen anyone, Ivy". No lady had passed him. Ivy went as white as a sheet and had to sit in Robert's office to recover.

One evening my brother-in-law Barry, who was visiting the Castle, went to the loo in the kitchen. He came back quite dazed and as white as a sheet. He said he'd seen a ghost as he went into the kitchen. "I'm never coming back here again", he said, and he never did. He said it was someone in dark clothes.

There are also some comments from Pat Withers (then Hayes) quoted in the 6th Earl's book *Ermine Tales*. In 1964 Pat and her father were decorating the long passageway that leads from the back door to the cellars – this is the oldest part of the Castle. One evening she was working near the kitchen door and her father was outside the servants' hall (now the first tea room). Pat heard her father say: "Good evening" to someone and, puzzled as to who it might be, she turned to look. Seeing no one she presumed that whoever it was had walked in the opposite direction. She carried on until her father angrily accused her of failing to greet the lady he'd seen. He explained that a tall lady dressed in black had walked down the stairs going in Pat's direction. No such person had passed Pat and there was no one, staff or guests, staying in the Castle who bore the slightest resemblance to Mr Hayes' description. Could this have been the ghost of old Lady Carnarvon whose baby had died in the nursery, or the nanny who was blamed for the death? No one knows.

SPOOKS AROUND THE HOUSE...

When mediums visited Highclere, one saw dogs in the front hall, small dogs with an old man sitting on the seat to the right of the door leading into the Library. There was also an old man sitting in a chair in the saloon. In the passage corridor just outside the brush room there was a lady walking down the corridor. There was a very strong presence of children. Outside the coal store/wine cellars there was a strong force, with considerable energy also felt outside the Egyptian Exhibition. I said it was the electricity power box but it was definitely recording on their energy meter as well – no one could deny it.

I have worked through the night at Highclere, both on my own and with people. I have often walked down the long passage in the dark to my bedroom via the servants' stairs, but I have never seen anyone. The only experience that I've had in all my 32 years at Highclere happened at about 10pm one evening, and this story was published in America. I was polishing the long passage and then buffing it. This was after we'd opened to the public. I had reached the brush room near the tea rooms when suddenly I heard a loud bang and a rattling of doors. It was then that the fire doors opened and closed, then slowly opened and closed again and a breeze hit me.

If you've ever been to Highclere Castle, you'll know the fire doors are half-way down the corridor. No breeze could have pushed those doors open. Yes, a breeze could have caused the next set of doors to rattle, but if you push the fire doors they are so heavy there is no way this could have happened. At that time Tony, my husband, was standing at the back door knocking and he saw them open too. When I went down to see him he said: "I'm off, what are you going to do?" "I must finish the corridor", I said. Admittedly it was weird but I don't believe in ghosts so I thought there had to be some reasonable explanation. It makes you wonder, though, doesn't it?

Laurence Udell, a very stable young man, was at the Castle for a period of 4 months working on Mercury Communications' seminars and teambuilding events. He asked to see me in one of the rooms that they were using. "Maureen, if you ever frighten me like that again, you and I will not be friends any more". Quite taken aback, I told him I'd been in the Library with the rest of my team for the past hour clearing up. He related what had happened to him. From the Gents' loo he went up the small staircase leading to the offices, because they used those rooms in their programme. Someone followed him and all the hairs on the back of his neck stood up; a cold, uneasy feeling went through his body but he saw no one. He thought I was playing a joke on him, which is what we used to do, but for once I wasn't guilty. Was this the ghost of old Lady Carnarvon going to her bedroom? Believe me, he took it very seriously indeed and never went up the staircase again once he realised it wasn't me.

East Anglia bedroom at Highclere has often been the subject of debate concerning ghosts. Seances were held in this room when the 6th Earl was alive. A séance was filmed in East Anglia for part of the film *The Missionary*, which dealt with the 5th and 6th Earls' interest in the past life. The 7th Earl and Countess of Carnarvon always felt a presence when they stayed at Highclere for a year while Milford Lake was undergoing alteration and refurbishment following their marriage. In my time at Highclere this room always felt cold, even though electric heaters were on for most of the time, summer and winter. There were often indentations on the pillows and the top covers, even when the doors were kept locked. In theory this room should have been warm as it benefited from the afternoon sun to the south. Very odd!

...and in the garden

Pat Withers had another bad experience when working on the young carnation greenhouse in the top gardens. It had a tall hedge and Pat had her ladders resting near the hedge. She was at the top of the ladder when she heard footsteps – this was around 8pm so everyone should have been at dinner in the Castle. Pat thought it was his Lordship with his guests. "Blimey", she thought, "Ivy's going to be mad if all the guests are down here". No one materialized but the footsteps still continued where Pat was working, went around her ladder and carried on. Pat saw no one. She quickly came down from the ladder, left everything as it was and went home. Next day Jock Reid, the head gardener, asked Pat what the matter was as she'd left the paint pot, brush and all her equipment just as it was. Pat said: "I'm never working down this garden on my own again", and told him what had happened. This prompted Jock to tell Pat of his experience near the statue of Charlemagne in the garden. He'd heard a baby crying many times but could never find it or discover what the problem was.

Dave Radwell, who was head gamekeeper to the 6th Earl at the time, was coming down Lime Avenue on his way home. He saw a woman in old-fashioned clothes pushing an old pram with a baby in it and some dogs in tow. She was walking towards his pheasant pens so he turned around thinking: "God, if those dogs get near the pens all hell will be let loose". When he got there, there was no one to be seen. He asked the men cutting down trees at the top of the Avenue but no one had seen anything.

The Queen at Highclere

My first glimpse of The Queen came when I worked for the 6th Earl. The scullery of the kitchen faced the stables and the courtyard. As I looked out of the window I caught sight of a couple entering the stables. To my dismay they headed for the kitchen, so I went inside, found Ivy and brought her to the window. She looked and said, "Don't worry, it's The Queen and Lord Porchester [later the 7th Earl] wandering around."

"The Queen!" I said. "You're kidding." "No", replied Ivy.

She was dressed in an old Barbour coat, headscarf and wellies. Ivy said "Maureen, The Queen often comes to Milford Lake. She and the Carnarvons are great friends". What I hadn't realised was that The Queen also needed to relax and unwind. She shared the same passion for horses and horseracing as the Carnarvon family.

The 7th Earl became The Queen's racing manager in 1969 and held that position until he died in 2001. During my early years at Highclere I encountered her only twice. After the 6th Earl died, the 7th Earl used the Castle for many of his private functions, such as shooting parties. We had a shooting book that was used to keep records of who attended. Prince Philip always signed the book, using the address of W.C. (Windsor Castle). When The Queen signed the book she would always sign it Elizabeth R. On the 7th Earl's shoots she would always take the opportunity to relax, often entering the front hall full of enthusiasm, taking off her wellies and showing her shooting socks. They were blue with silvery threads, a Christmas present from one of her grandchildren.

On those days The Queen would help pick up the birds for the guns although she didn't actually shoot herself. Sometimes Prince Philip and Prince Charles would also come to the Castle and attend shoots. When they had a chocolate rum soufflé I remember Prince Charles wondering aloud how far they had to dig to find the rum.

As the housekeeper I was the one to look after The Queen and escort her to East Anglia where she could freshen up before lunch. After a few minutes I would feel quite at ease because she was so natural with people and began talking about the day's shoot and her corgis. One particular day there had been thunderstorm after thunderstorm. As we were coming down the stairs we could hear Lord Carnarvon laughing and I remarked how good it was to hear him sounding so jolly; someone must have told an excellent joke. But it was then that we saw water running down the windows on the staircase, making a dreadful mess. "Lord Carnarvon won't be laughing when he hears about this", I said. The Queen replied: "I had a fire at Windsor Castle so I had lots of repairs done!"

Lord Carnarvon went shooting in atrocious weather conditions to avoid losing face with Prince Philip. They came in for lunch on one occasion and someone remarked that Lord Carnarvon was soaked right through to his underpants. Prince Philip asked his loaders whether they should go out after lunch; they told him he shouldn't even attempt it and Lord Carnarvon must be mad if he went out.

When The Queen came on special occasions things were rather different because she was acting in her official capacity as Head of State. Police searched the Castle with sniffer dogs highly trained to uncover explosives. However, there was the time one young dog wee'd all over the carpet in the Herbert bedroom, so accidents happen, even with the most expertly tutored animals. East Anglia bedroom became The Queen's dressing room; it was one of her favourites because of the view over the grounds. Once it had been screened it was locked and a policewoman assigned to sit outside as part of the security procedure until Her Majesty needed to use it.

A fleet of unmarked police cars was always on hand inside the grounds when she was visiting, so it was pretty obvious she was there. She came to Lady Carolyn and John Warren's wedding with Princess Diana and Prince Andrew. She also attended Harry and Chica's wedding with Princess Diana. For the wedding of her godson Geordie, then Lord Porchester (now the 8th Earl), The Queen attended with Princess Margaret.

During the time that Harry and Chica ran the Castle, The Queen and Queen Mother were looking at the yearlings at Highclere Stud. Wesuddenly had a phone call saying that they'd both be coming for a tour. The Queen had only been to shoots and functions and had never actually had a good look round, while the Queen Mother had never visited at all. We talked about the oak in the saloon and how long I'd been at Highclere. I waited on one side as Lord Carnarvon took them into the dining room. As Lord Carnarvon talked about the famous painting of Charles I, The Queen commented to his Lordship: "Oh yes, but I have the original". Classic, I thought. After they had done their tour I was introduced and Harry took photographs of us all. I was thrilled and honoured when I was presented with a print.

Racing

Horse racing affected my life during my time at Highclere, not because of The Queen but because of the achievements of the Carnarvon family. When cleaning the Racing Exhibition the gold, silver and crystal trophies had to be looked after and that was my responsibility. The Carnarvons have enjoyed more than their share of success on the turf and have always loved horses and racing. I could reel off all the trophies they have won and all the famous horses they have owned and bred, but unless you are a racing fan the names will not mean anything.

I remember when Lake Coniston won for Highclere Thoroughbred Racing, Harry broke down in tears. He was simply showing appreciation for all the dedication and hard work his team had put in. There are syndicates that support H.T.R. and Harry throughout the year, especially at the yearling parades which are held at the stud and Castle.

John Warren, The Queen's current racing manager, has a rare talent when it comes to bloodstock and runs Highclere Stud with his wife, Lady Carolyn. I saw my first foal being born there and it was exhilarating, not merely because it came from good stock but because it was a new life. One day it would give pleasure to racegoers when it surged across the winning line. There would be triumph, glory and laughter for some, and tears for those who failed to bet on a star performer. The few times I have been to the races, at Royal Ascot and Newbury, brought some of the happiest moments of my life. I can appreciate top quality horseflesh.

JUNE 4th 2005

Harry and John Warren formed Royal Ascot Racing Management and achieved the perfect result when Motivator ran away with the Epsom Derby in 2005. He cost only 75,000 guineas, which is very cheap indeed these days, and turned out to be one of the bargains of all time. As I say, John Warren is an outstanding judge of a yearling.

Tutankhamun artefacts and Highclere

The 5th Earl of Carnarvon is always mentioned in connection with the discovery of the tomb of Tutankhamun, of course, and there are many magnificent Egyptian artefacts at Highclere as a result.

THE EGYPTIAN WEEKEND

Nick Reeves, an Egyptologist and archaeologist who, together with his wife Claire, worked extensively on the collection of artefacts found in the Castle, organised an Egyptian weekend which delegates from around the world attended. The 7th Earl kindly helped by making the Castle available for the seminars. Evening receptions and dinners were included as part of the event and many things were of Egyptian orientation. The Queen donated part of her Egyptian collection for the weekend. Nick was in the Castle's Egyptian room when I walked in to look at the collection. Of all the wonderful pieces there, the things that impressed me most of all were two cats. He showed me inside the mummified cats and there were these small pieces of rag – it was amazing.

I couldn't understand why the small collection belonging to The Queen couldn't have been on display to the general public and advertised accordingly, but it wasn't to be. Fortunately, the display remained open longer than originally intended and a few lucky people saw it, although the Castle was not allowed to publicise the collection. A great deal of hard work went into organising the weekend. Claire, for example, had recreated the remainder of an Egyptian shroud that was on display. The occasion was a great success and the Carnarvons were very fortunate to have been part of it all.

Les Taylor and I tried to spin Nick a yarn on opening. Les had done his homework on Egyptology signs and told Nick a story about all the wooden pieces we'd thrown out into the skip, describing them in great detail. Nick was getting so frustrated that when he'd had nearly an hour of it we finally let him in on the joke. It was so convincing he didn't believed Les when he found the calcite head in the old golf bag in the brush room – but it was a genuine discovery this time.

Nick stayed on as curator for a few years while expanding his knowledge, which affected his marriage and family life. Some would say it was the curse of 'old Tutankhamun', while others would say that was complete nonsense.

THE CURSE OF 'OLD TUT'?
Here are a few examples of things ending unhappily.

- Lady Almina (whom I met) was the 5th Earl's wife and suffered constantly from poor health. She eventually ended her days in Switzerland.
- Lady Evelyn Beecham, the 5th Earl's sister, was a frequent visitor to Highclere but she, too, suffered from poor health.
- Bill Misson, the 6th Earl's valet and chauffeur, died of leukaemia.

Nor was ill health the only bad luck. Marriages, too, seemed ill-fated. During my time at Highclere, the 6th Earl had been divorced twice. The 8th Earl's first wife, Lady Jane Porchester, was rumoured to have run off with the captain of the South African cricket team. This rumour was spread to discredit her but was unsubstantiated. The 8th Earl finally divorced her when he was still Lord Porchester. The other failed marriages at Highclere included:

- Nick Reeves and his wife Claire, as mentioned above.
- Eddie and Jennie Hughes: head keeper to the 7th and 8th Earl
- Martin and Lindsey Giles: forester and co-ordinator/secretary to the 7th and 8th Earl.
- Mandy and Chris Marfleet: banqueting staff to the 7th Earl.
- Mark and Angela Greenfield: head chef to the 7th Earl.
- Maureen and Tony Cummins: housekeeper and house manager to the 7th Earl.
- Jackie and Derek Lessware: secretary to the 7th and 8th Earl.

Was it the pressure of work, or simply coincidence? Divorces, failed marriages, ill health, were all these part of 'old Tutankhamun's curse?

Opportunities lost

Adrian could have made the Carnarvons millions by recreating the Egyptian Tomb of Tutankhamun at Highclere in the old icehouse. Highclere would have been the Egypt of Great Britain. He would have turned the courtyard into Victorian workshops for educational purposes. The idea was so original and imaginative it was unbelievable that the 7th Earl opposed it: how short-sighted they all were. The reason, of course, was that the family simply would not have their privacy invaded. Well, that was fine if they'd actually lived at Highclere, but they were far enough away on the estate for it not be a factor. Another idea discussed – and opposed – was that of extending the Egyptian rooms in the Castle cellars. This would have taken them into the champagne cellar, then down past the flower room. What a fantastic idea! So many brilliant ideas received no support and there is only so much a person can take before asking: "Why do I bother? What's the point? There's no support from the family".

Shooting

Shooting was the 6th Earl's great love, together with golf and racing. This meant that he would entertain his friends with fine wines, then wonderful, high-quality shooting – which Highclere always excelled at and still does.

If I were asked which season of the year I enjoyed at Highclere most, I would say from September to the end of January – the shooting season. When the 6th Earl entertained, the food was always of the highest quality – lobster, crab, turbot, leg of lamb, fillet of beef, Dover sole, salmon. Even when he had cottage pie it was always made with the best leg of lamb. It was always the best of everything. All the vegetables were home grown so everything you could wish for was fresh. It all came from the kitchen garden, together with fresh fruits of the season. Fresh peaches, plums, nectarines, raspberries, strawberries and redcurrants all came from the gardens.

Mark Sanderson had his own dairy herd next to the gardens so fresh milk and cream were available. Johnny Collins, Ivy's brother, helped Mark and then, when Mark died and the farm and herd were sold, Johnny went to help on the estate and later became part of the gardening team. Fresh ice cream was made by hand (that's why I have such strong muscles in my arms). If you could see me you'd understand why I've always had a problem with my weight. Whilst cooking I lived on the best of everything, as we all did.

During the shooting season the staff would live in; ladies maids, chauffeurs, loaders, they too experienced the 6th Earl's hospitality. One loader came and used to love the Stilton. After the loaders, lunch you could see his pockets bulging with goodies that he was taking home. To me this went a bit far and eventually he was accosted by Les Taylor, head of security.

The 6th Earl's dogs (retired) lived with Ivy while his black tailed labrador, Prune, always stayed in the Castle kitchen. The dogs were always given all the scraps but one day Prune thought she'd go one better and pinched a leg of lamb from the kitchen table. Ivy was furious but Prune just sat licking her lips.

Eddie Hughes started work on the estate at 14. At that time you could leave school if you had a job to go to. He stayed for 3 years then left for a couple of years to pursue other interests. When he came back he helped the keepers and later became assistant to the head keeper. Eddie married Jenny Oakley, a housemaid at Highclere, in 1972. He became head keeper after Dave Radwell's redundancy and remains head keeper to this day. He remembers some amusing stories from the shoots, especially the story of Bill Misson's hat:

Friday: While loading for the 6th Earl at Blenheim Palace, the Duke of Marlborough (Bertie) cut the shoot short owing to pouring rain. It was decided to shoot ducks from the Grand Bridge instead. Bill Misson, the 6th Earl's valet, saw everyone and went to join them. The Duke said to Misson: "Where's your hat, it's pouring!" Misson replied: "I haven't got one, your Grace".

Saturday: A glorious day for a shoot. The Duke saw Misson with a hat on. "Oh, I see you've a hat on today, Misson". Misson replied: "Yes, and thank you, your Grace, for it". "What do you mean?" his Grace said as he stopped dead on the Palace steps. Misson said: "I went into Woodstock and got a hat and put it on your account, your Grace". You should have seen the look on his Grace's face! "Some people have the cheek of the devil", he muttered as he stormed off. Eddie and Fred Bramble the Duke's valet looked on astounded but chuckled to think Misson had had the last laugh. Which was typical of him.

GUNS WHO ATTENDED THE 6TH EARL OF CARNAVON'S SHOOTS
Prince Philip
Prince Charles
Lord Derby

Lord Tavistock
Lord Sefton
Colonel Stirling
Mr Parrington
Major Rose
Major Mills
Hugh Williams
Gerritt van de Woude
David van de Woude
Michael van de Woude
Lady Penelope
Katherine van de Woude

Mary Povey, Lord Carnarvon's secretary, used to prepare the Game Cards in January and they always said: "It is a far cry to the next season". Then he'd sign them on his return from Nasser six weeks later.

On a shoot at Highclere, guests of the 6th Earl included Captain Mark Phillips, Princess Anne, Jackie Stewart and others. Mark Phillips was on the 6th Earl's left, Jackie Stewart on the right and Princess Anne was sitting on the fence. The 6th Earl was desperate for a pee. Eddie Hughes was loading for his Lordship. "You can't go here, my Lord". "Why not?" said the 6th Earl. "We have guests, my Lord", said Eddie. His Lordship said to Eddie, "Lord Derby once told me: 'Those that haven't seen it, want to see it, and those who have seen it want to see it more.' Now take this fucking gun". He then proceeded to hand the gun to Eddie and went to have a pee in front of the guests.

The 6th Earl always liked to go grouse shooting in Scotland on or after the Glorious Twelfth – the first day of the grouse shooting season. My first encounter with grouse came when I arrived in September, 1968. The 6th Earl loved grouse highly seasoned, which meant a really strong smell. It used to turn my stomach when plucking and preparing it and I couldn't understand anyone eating such a bird – it was definitely not my favourite. Partridge was a different matter, I would certainly have given my right arm for one but we were not allowed any. It wasn't until years later that I tasted some and found it wonderful. The 6th Earl also loved woodcock but, when I saw how they were cooked, my initial thought was that they were disgusting. Everything was left inside, then cooked and drawn out on to the toast so that the entrails soaked in. This was a delicacy and enjoyed to the full. I decided to give it a miss.

Quails and percolin were obtained from a farm at Whitway which hand-reared them. For many years percolin was on the menu but it wasn't until 1999 that I discovered that there was no such bird. Adrian Wiley and I had a bet one day and, as I thought it was a dead cert, the prize was a bottle of Puligny Montrachet. That was fine by me and I wrote to the RSPB to get all the information on this bird, still convinced that I was going to win as it had been on the menu for years. Ivy Collins and I had cooked them and there were menus written for dinners that the 6th Earl had hosted. Mary Povey had collected them on her way to work. The letter I received back from the RSPB said there was no such bird. You could have knocked me down with a feather (I still have the menus and letter). I paid my debt but couldn't believe that all those years we'd been cooking and serving percolin yet there was no such bird. My, didn't we have a good laugh about it! I believe the word may have derived from the French, but there was no way of proving that percolin existed in English.

The 6th Earl didn't have too many pheasant and preferred them casseroled unless they were very young, in which case he had them roasted with thinly-sliced American bacon on top. He had the bacon brought over specially from the States, though nowadays you can obtain it quite easily in this country. It always fascinated me when the pheasants came back from Chester-le-Street in County Durham where the 6th Earl went shooting. They all had a beautiful double layer of feathers. Nature was wonderful and really looked after her pheasants.

When we hosted a simulated game shoot at Highclere for Imperial Tobacco, I made a bit of a faux pas. The policy for events held at Highclere was 'no smoking' and I commented both to Wendy Plummer, the organiser, and Peter

Middleton that they were setting cigarettes out for guests arriving in the saloon and dining room. In panic I said, "You can't do that, don't you know that we have a 'no smoking' policy at Highclere?" The uproar must have been heard everywhere. Wendy stormed off to find Adrian Wiley, the Castle manager. He proceeded to sort out the situation and explained to them and to me that sometimes we had to waive the rules, especially when the client was Imperial Tobacco or the House of Lords. What more could I say?

The tradition of the shooting lunches carried on through the 7th Earl's time. Fortunately Geordie, the 8th Earl of Carnarvon, who inherited the title in September 2001 from his dear Pa, is a great shot so everything should continue in the same way. After 32 years of being involved in the house I'd never actually been on a shoot so (as I mentioned earlier) during my last few months at Highclere, which happened to fall during the shooting season, I was asked to do some loading on a shoot that Marco Pierre White, the famous chef, was hosting. I was bubbling with excitement all day.

SHOOT DAYS

Breakfast:
Breakfast on shoot days consisted of a very large York ham with kidneys, kippers, American and Danish bacon, two types of eggs, tomatoes, mushrooms, plenty of toast, salmon or haddock kedgeree. Breakfast was always an enormous affair and really not to be missed. Many of the lady guests would have trays upstairs and one in particular, who was a very firm favourite of the 6th Earl, Countess Esterhazy (Bunnie), would have freshly boiled eggs. Our instructions in the kitchen were to put the eggs in cold water, bring to the boil and boil for one minute, then put the egg cosy on. Mrs Reid then took them up two flights of stairs and, just outside the bedroom before her tray was presented, she tapped the top of the egg. Two eggs perfectly done – it never failed. This is why Countess Esterhazy shot as well as she did – her perfection matched the eggs!

Mid morning – taken out to the shoot:
Hot homemade soup and vodka or a tot of sloe gin.

Pre-lunch drinks

Bloody Marys, gin and tonic or anything from the bar

Lunch

Three-course lunch. Steak & kidney pudding, stew or Navarin of lamb or many other alternatives, then a pudding ranging from a steamed pudding, a wholesome treacle tart or apple tart, always followed by cheese and port. It made you wonder if they'd have the energy to shoot, but neither the food nor the weather ever prevented them. Two hours later, back for tea.

Tea

A cup of tea and a homemade fruit cake.

Dinner

Dinner in the evening always consisted of three to four courses, together with wines.

Art and music at Highclere

PAUL HODGES

Paul studied at Sheffield University and passed his Art degree with full honours, an added benefit, no doubt, of falling in love with and marrying his course lecturer Anne Greby, by which time they were having their first baby together, a daughter. I met Paul at Highclere when he came to talk about paintings with Adrian, who had engaged him as artist in residence at Harewood House, the great 18th Century stately home in Yorkshire. He was a carefree individual at the time and very talented with it. He will never be rich but, like most artists, will always get by. That sublime ability to create paintings based on things that have happened in his life is something that comes from the soul. His instinctive rapport with nature enables him to capture peace and tranquillity but also the destruction caused by man that many do not see.

Once a happy man, Paul knew disappointment in affairs of the heart in faraway lands, his unhappiness showing clearly enough in a painting of the women in his life. Visits to different continents taught him about the jungle and the rain forest and a new way of life became apparent in his work. A substantial commission for a new hotel, Newbury Manor, put enormous pressure on him. This might have been the height of his career but he was, perhaps, too relaxed and easy-going for a task which required constant self-motivation. With deadlines approaching the pressure increased and Paul found the burden weighing heavily on his shoulders, turning him into a more aggressive person. Help in the person of his wife (now his ex-wife) Anne, an artist in her own right, was required in order to meet the deadline and relieve the strain brought on by this daunting task, which was to create a masterpiece for the dining room incorporating all the beauty surrounding the hotel. Paul was a wonderful artist whose talent touched perfection at times, but his God-given ability was stretched to the outer limit on this occasion. He eventually completed the task, but at what cost? Anne, shortly after her visit to the Castle, decided to abandon him as a result of his liaison with a Russian girl when he was part of Operation Raleigh.

Since then Paul has had a few commissions abroad. His Egyptian collection, painted while he was artist-in-residence at Highclere, shows the true quality of his work whilst also reflecting his life and experiences. He should have received the equivalent of an Oscar. Occasionally Paul would help me with the cleaning in the Castle and he also attended functions. On one occasion he was even a witness at a wedding. He was in love with the beauty of things and sometimes found it very hard, wasting his time on routine jobs. On the surface his cheerfulness and relaxed attitude made him appear a warm, amiable person, but the intensity of his inner feelings also shone through when he expressed himself on canvas.

His artistry in a commercial environment might not have excited the world at large but, for a collector with an eye for perfection, he had the touch of a modern genius. I am proud to know him and to have had him working with me for a short while. His is a rare talent, pure and free. I believe he is in a class of his own.

THE RUSSIAN ARTISTS
I met the Russian artists Valery and Katya Gridnev through the craft fair at Highclere Castle. Their work was on display in a tent called 'Artists from Russia'. As I entered, a painting of a small boy sitting at a piano next to his teacher or mother stood out among all the others. It was a sad picture but magnificent in every way. The following year there was one of two boys sitting on a bench outside a building, as well as pictures of ballerinas and some scenes with fishing boats. These had to be the same artists, clearly very talented, and I fell in love with the paintings straightaway. The ballerinas had been caught in their true, natural state. I didn't realise then that the artists would play a great part in my life.

Valery was born in the Russian Urals in 1956 and studied at Sverdlovsk Art College, after which he spent seven years at the St Petersburg Academy of Arts. He took the advancement course of studies at the USSR Academy of Arts. For his graduation painting Early Years he won the prestigious Gold Medal. From 1990 to 1994 he worked in the creative studio, again at the St Petersburg Academy. Since 1991 he has been a member of the Russian Artists, Federation. With his wife Katya and son Feodor he moved to England in 1999. Katya was born in the Ukraine in 1965 and also studied at the St Petersburg Academy of Arts. She has exhibited her work in Germany, Moscow and London. Katya and Valery work closely together, often simultaneously on portrait commissions, which highlights a delightful similarity in their work. Since living in England both artists have been very successful indeed.

Valery, Katya and Feodor came to Highclere Castle. They were a very talented family who spoke little English but I warmed to them immediately. Adrian gave them a great deal of support as he'd known them a lot longer than I and had bought some of their earlier paintings of ballerinas. Their artistic flair was quite different from that of Paul Hodges; a certain freedom of spirit flowed gracefully through their work. Yearning for success in a new country, they were inspired to keep on painting. Like Paul, who paints to live but is still a genius, they are of a different class.

With Adrian's help they rented my bungalow in Hurstbourne Tarrant, then a house nearer Newbury for Feodor's schooling. Individual commissions to paint the 7th Earl and Countess of Carnarvon, Chica Herbert and her children and the 8th Earl made them more successful. A pastel of Lester Piggott in Highclere Thoroughbred Racing colours raised a considerable sum for a well-known charity, while the 7th Earl's friend, the Earl of Ripon, had an oil painting commissioned. Many galleries in London show their work, and Valery and Katya have also held private exhibitions in both London and America. They are a warm, kind family who have always made me feel welcome. Their success is down to native ability, hard work and the help of a few friends. They lived in Oxford for a while as Feodor won a scholarship there and was studying for an art degree. He has inherited their sublime talent and is also fluent in three languages.

I once rushed Valery to Winchester Hospital as Katya couldn't drive at the time. He had a problem with his pacemaker and it needed urgent attention. They have recently moved to London for the sake of their son's education. How fortunate I am to have been part of their life and helped them in some way. I wish them health and prosperity in the years to come.

JOACHIM RAFF

My determination to have the music of Raff played live took a few years to achieve, but I finally made it. During an evening at the Newbury Spring Festival, I approached John Wright, the artistic director, with an LP of Raff's Fifth Symphony and he was very interested. I sent him a tape recording and he was intrigued enough to say he'd try to get it orchestrated. We needed £20,000 to fund the project and John had to bring together an orchestra and a conductor and start organising sponsorship. Many times I tried to have Raff played on Classic FM but without success.

Over a period of time John Wright managed to interest John Boydon, artistic director to the New Queen Hall Orchestra. A tough challenge was in store, with grit and determination needed. I set myself the task of raising £2,000 by ironing shirts at £1.00 per shirt; this seemed a brilliant idea at the time! I tried to get sponsorship from different people but no one was really interested. As this piece of music was new it was difficult to get hold of a conductor but finally Paul Murphy agreed to take it on. My dream finally came true on the 25th June 2002 in the Holy Trinity Church, Sloane Square, when the piece was played at the Chelsea Festival. John Wright had been true to his word.

The programme was:
>   Rossini   William Tell Overture
>   Raff   Fifth Symphony
>   Widor   Solo Organ
>   Saint-Saens Third Symphony.

Radio Berkshire, the International Herald Tribune and Newbury Weekly News were among those who interviewed me about my achievement. What a fabulous evening it had been! But all the credit should go to John Wright, who made my dream come true. I shall be forever indebted to him.

Vivid memories of the film world

1986 was a wonderful year for Highclere because the motion picture *The Secret Garden* was filmed in its entirety there. Norman Rosemont, the producer, chose Highclere from many houses for this famous film, of which many adaptations have been made for television. We had many stars there, Billie Whitelaw, Michael Hordern, Julian Glover, Tony Selby and Alison Doody among them. The overall timing for this film, set entirely on location at Highclere, took up a period of 9 to 10 weeks. The action was scheduled mainly for the middle six weeks but everything had to be organised around the awful weather we had at the time, which certainly didn't make life easy.

Highclere was Mistlewaithe Manor in Yorkshire and the home of Mr Craven. The Georgian part of Highclere's courtyard was transformed to look like a scene from India during the plague. My house, which backed on to the courtyard, was blocked out with wooden blinds for the purpose of this film. As it was so dark I was given £100 towards my electricity bill. As the carriage approached the Castle it looked like snow, but in fact it was rock salt from every DIY store in Newbury!

The Secret Garden was created near Jackdaws Castle on the far left. It took weeks to construct and eventually had to go through the four seasons of the year with the help of an enormous wind machine. They had a tame fox for one of the scenes and it escaped. Believe me, the keepers were not amused because it was near the pheasant pens.

Mary's bedroom was arranged in East Anglia and Colin's was portrayed in Stanhope. Even the church at Newtown Common was used. The Victorian kitchen played an important part in the film because of its size; also, it still had the huge stove and brasses used in that period. At the time the 6th Earl was in a nursing home at Woolton Hill, which made the creation of this magnificent film rather more straightforward that it would otherwise have been.

Norman Rosemont returned in August 1999 to film part of *The Return to the Secret Garden* and he was delighted to see me again. Robert Taylor had died in 1990 but he still remembered him. Times change, of course, and commercialism is now a vital factor where supporting the Castle is concerned. It would be truly wonderful to have another great film produced at Highclere, although I don't think there could ever be one as marvellous as *The Secret Garden*. It captured perfectly the Victorian era when Highclere was in its pomp.

A few shots of *Blott on the Landscape* were filmed at Highclere and also *The Free Frenchman*. Les Taylor's labrador Flaggs appeared in this version and was quite a star. *Heirs & Graces* came to Highclere in 1989 with Lady Victoria Leatham and John Bly. This was the first full year that we'd been open to the public but our second season. Lady Leatham was fascinated by the Gothic look and the George Gilbert Scott design of the front hall and the colouring of William Butterfield's marble floor. During a walkabout through the old nursery she discovered two rare 18th century Worcester vases and she and Robert relocated them in the red hall outside the smoking room. This was a genuine discovery and, even though one of them was chipped, Lady Leatham was adamant that they should be displayed. John Bly was fascinated by the Bullock side cabinets in the dining room. George Bullock had put the marble on to Welsh slate that came from his quarry in Anglesey.

In 1989 Jason Connery and Patricia Hodge also came to film at Highclere. They were involved in making parts of *The Secret Life of Ian Fleming*. Quite a lot took place in the Queen Caroline bedroom and on the third floor of the old nursery. Unfortunately this caused a bit of a stir with the lighting crew. The huge lights had to be hauled up three flights of stairs, as did the dolly to hold the huge camera that they used in those days. Eventually, after a great deal of thought, the film crew came up trumps and filming continued.

In March 1990 Edward Woodward played Sherlock Holmes, Anthony Andrews was Moriarty and the American actor John Hillerman (Butler in Hawaii Five O) played Watson in *The Hands of a Murderer*. The film cost £5m to make for CBS American TV and Yorkshire TV. The outside of my home, the garages and Day's Cottage as well as the cemetery were used.

Later that year Alison Doody and Billie Whitelaw returned to make parts of *Duel of Love*, which starred Michael York and Benedict Taylor. The film was later retitled *Duel of Hearts*, based on a Barbara Cartland book. During filming Leslie Phillips popped in to see everyone; he was really jolly and so much fun. In June 1990 the gardens were the setting for the opening of *King Ralph I*. Scenes were also shot in the main Library. John Hurt starred in this film and one of the scenes had him smoking by the Carlton House desk. No one had told the Castle staff. We all knew that John Hurt was a heavy smoker and, after much debate, he was allowed to continue.

Also in 1990, parts of the epic medieval adventure *Robin Hood – Prince of Thieves* were filmed in the grounds of Highclere. The film starred Kevin Costner, Morgan Freeman and Mary Elizabeth Mastrantonio amongst others. John Mason was the estate's maintenance man. Anything that needed fixing, he'd fix it. I'd just finished my morning shift at the Castle when he shouted to me and asked if I'd like a lift to the temple as he had to go and do some repairs on the bridge – or so he said. I jumped into his van and off we went. Riding though the park was always a pleasure. As we turned off towards the temple (which is one of the follies on the estate) John asked me if I knew about Robin Hood. "Everyone knows about Robin Hood", I replied. "Yes, Mo, but not everyone has been on a film set of *Robin Hood – Prince of Thieves*, have they?" That's where we were going, and you could have knocked me down with a feather.

Apparently, parts of the film were being shot around the temple and the lake. Approaching the temple along the rough and winding roads I could see in the distance a great deal of activity. As we parked near the catering wagon a group of dirty peasants appeared to be queuing for their lunch. We wandered around until John found the person he'd come to see. It seemed they needed part of the wagon that he'd taken delivery of to do some repairs. We were introduced to the location manager and told we could have lunch and wander around while there was a break in filming. It was amazing – like being transported in the Tardis back to the 11th Century. Mist was creeping over the lake as we approached. Mist! It was a clear day and around lunchtime. Mist usually came over early in the morning in November. Finally the penny dropped. A team of people were trying out smoke machines, creating mist over the temple lake for a scene in the film where Kevin Costner (Robin Hood) puts Marion (Mary Elizabeth Mastrantonio) into a makeshift boat to make her escape.

Tracks were made on the film set for the dolly to travel on. This was where the action and filming took place. The cameraman would sit on the dolly to give him more mobility and cause less interruption on the set itself. It looked like a small railway track with a moveable seat on wheels, with an expanding arm for the camera. A big wooden wagon was positioned on a ramp, ready to be launched into the lake. It looked like it was held by large elastic arms ready to be catapulted into the sky, not the lake, but I was assured everything was timed and placed for the right effect. It was really amazing, but in the film itself they scrapped that particular scene and kept to Maid Marion floating into the mist on her boat.

We wandered back to the top of the hill to have lunch with the peasants. How authentic they looked; make-up and wardrobe had done an excellent job, they even smelled like peasants, with matted hair, ragged clothes and mud caked to their skin, right down to their finger nails. A mud bath couldn't have done the job better. Consequently we only stayed for a cuppa.

A mobile catering unit could take care of 70 to 100 personnel for lunch, which was taken in a converted double-decker red London bus. Even in the film industry there was a pecking order in the queue depending on how important you were. Three hot meals and a cold buffet were provided along with a great choice of puddings. A catering unit worked just as hard as the crew, and a well-fed crew was a contented crew. John and I pottered around, taking in the ambience of our surroundings. How lovely just to be present while a great film was in production. Unfortunately I didn't get to see Kevin Coster – just unlucky, I guess.

I had a wonderful time with Stephen Fry and Hugh Laurie during the time they filmed *Jeeves & Wooster* at Highclere. Three episodes were made there, in October 1990, September 1991 and October 1992. Hugh Laurie often played the piano but the best moment came when ten of the crew lifted the Steinway piano from the North Library to the Main Library. Rather a dramatic squeeze through the pillars, believe me! Hugh Laurie was so pleased that he played the piano to say thank you to everyone. Ferdinand Fairfax directed most of these episodes and was always known for his saying: 'Just one more time'. He was a brilliant director. Parts of *Jeeves & Wooster* were filmed during the public opening days and everyone was very curious, not minding at all when told to be quiet as the cameras were rolling and filming was in progress. The visitors simply loved it. In the last episode a huge marquee was erected for a big ball to take place. The wind got up and the crew worked very hard to prevent it from blowing away. I vaguely remember that during one of the episodes everyone went on strike because the director was very slow. He was ousted and Ferdinand Fairfax was asked to come back and finish the filming.

Channel 4 financed a film that covered a year in the life of Highclere. The first six months had been filmed before Adrian Wiley arrived and the remaining six followed his appointment as Castle manager. He'd been taken on to transform the Castle into a profitable business. It was Adrian who finally thought of the title *High Stakes at Highclere*. What an education!

I'm afraid I gave him such a hard time for the first six months I didn't deserve his kind comments in my autograph book. If you recall the film you'll know why! He wrote: 'To an utterly divine "family heirloom"', clearly thinking that he'd inherited me with the job! We had a good few laughs about this although, heirloom or not, I'd nearly been sacked in the early months. Thank God I had a few friends or I'd certainly have been out of a job and my son would have suffered and not had the special bond with Highclere that he experienced during his growing years.

Commercials were also a big hit at Highclere. There was *Death in the Library*, *Hunt Clothes*, and the Red Label Tea advert for Canadian TV which was shot in the drawing room. The *Mega Truffle* ice cream advert was filmed in the music room and drawing room. But the commercial that remains one of my fondest memories was the VW advert for English and German Television in March 1995. Everything was as you saw it but in order to do the last shot they had to find a clear bulb. Everyone searched everywhere for a single bulb. Just imagine it: all those bulbs in the Castle and we couldn't find a clear one. In the end I brought one from home – I only had one anyway. Marvellous, isn't it!

The Flash advertisement with the uncle as the owner of a stately home was also filmed at Highclere. The advert was used to launch the new Flash wipes, the sales pitch focusing on their effectiveness and efficiency when cleaning the dirtiest and grimiest parts of the house. This really upset me as it made out that the Castle was extremely dirty, whereas I've always prided myself on my very high standards. I was told to cool it because it was only an advert, after all. Brilliant.

STANLEY KUBRICK AND *EYES WIDE SHUT*

I met many stars during my time at Highclere – Shirley Bassey and Sir Elton John to name but two – but I must say I was overwhelmed when I heard that Stanley Kubrick was coming to see if we might provide a suitable location for one of his films. We dressed in our best bib and tucker only to find that Kubrick came dressed very casually and in the oldest pair of trainers in existence. To me it was very encouraging as I love to be in trainers and I'd been told I couldn't wear mine! He was a very charming person, thoughtful and caring. He decided that Highclere was indeed a suitable location for part of the film *Eyes Wide Shut* – a film we were later to find out was an erotic sexual fantasy.

What a bonus it would be if Tom Cruise came along! Well, he did. What's more, he was very well thought of by all the film crew. Apparently he was very good to all of them and a joy to work with. He was a very charming and pleasant person but just before he arrived I was told by the crew not to look him straight in the eye or he'd get me sacked. I just laughed and said "Oh, don't worry, I've had so many people trying to sack me that I've got used to it by now and besides, I don't work for the film crew I work for the 7th Earl of Carnarvon". I don't know if they were winding my up but, just for the hell of it, I looked him straight in the eye and nothing happened. I just beamed at him and told him how pleased we were to welcome him to Highclere and what a pleasure it was to meet him. He replied: "Thanks, it's a pleasure to meet you too". We got on famously from that moment on. When he brought his adopted children, Connor and Isabelle, to the Castle to show them around, I greeted them at the front door. He came in, took them to one side and went down on one knee. He put his arms around each of them and gave them a good talking to, telling them how he expected them to behave when they were in Lord Carnarvon's home. He explained that I was the housekeeper and that if they misbehaved I would deal with them; then he winked at me and smiled.

Stanley Kubrick was known to be a perfectionist and he lived up to his reputation. One of the crew was politely asked to leave as he'd kicked the centre leg from a wooden couch in the saloon. Even though it was an accident he was still told to go as Kubrick stood no nonsense and had great respect for his environment. He thought the crew should feel that way, too. If he wanted to think, he'd make this gesture with his hands and everyone would have to go outside. He and Tom Cruise brought their own chef with them on location, while our chef at Highclere Castle catered for the film crew. One evening, to everyone's amazement, Kubrick asked for a little of the film crew's mulligatawny soup as it was a freezing cold night. Everyone found this very unusual because he only ever ate what his own chef cooked. Mark Greenfield, the chef at Highclere, was right chuffed! He is a fine chef and it was a great compliment to him. The thing that amazed us most, and which we never quite understood, was Kubrick's desire to have everything as normal, with no extra lighting. Blackouts were meant to be put across the windows, but often they never turned up and this went on for months.

Stanley and Tom had a very special bond. Kubrick was a bit eccentric but had great empathy with Tom. He would always think things through and make the script up as he went along. He worked to Californian time which was from

4.30pm until 6am the next day. One evening he just sat with Tom Cruise going over the way the film would look, just thinking it through. He'd thrown all of the crew into the freezing cold outside. I was in the Castle because I was the person taking care of the filming inside. Adrian Wiley took care of those outside, and they weren't much trouble apart from freezing themselves to death.

Adrian Wiley had told many guests and the 7th Earl that Stanley Kubrick and Tom Cruise were coming to film *Eyes Wide Shut*, but what he didn't know was that the film included a great deal of nudity and sexual activity. It came as a great shock to all of us, but it was all in a day's work. Anyway, what could we have done about it? Everything was signed and sealed with a contract in place. Adrian was sure he'd get his P45 because of the film, but he didn't. No one knew how erotic the scenes would be, certainly not Adrian, who was showing someone the smoking room when one of the actresses simply took her clothes off and walked on to the set absolutely naked!

During filming a new table was made for the sex scene on a dining table in the drawing room. I was present at many of these sex scenes but everyone just performed them naturally and professionally. They were all very cautious and discreet about the content of the film as Stanley Kubrick had the scripts made each day and the majority of the scenes at Highclere were action ones – and action speaks louder than words!

I took it as a great compliment when Stanley wrote a few words in my autograph book: '*To Maureen. Thank you for your great patience and help. Best wishes, Stanley Kubrick. 2nd February 1998*'. It was rare for him to sign anyone's book. I also have Tom Cruise's autograph but the most important one was Stanley Kubrick's. He was a great man and it was an honour to meet him. Sadly he died not all that long afterwards, which was a huge loss to the film world generally and Warner Brothers in particular. For *Eyes Wide Shut* they gave him unlimited funds, although it didn't turn into the blockbuster they'd hoped for.

FILM CREWS

Film crews came on recce visits several times before arriving on the day itself to start filming. We worked out several basic rules where crews were concerned, making sure we knew all about the following from the first recce.

a)   The type of film they were shooting.

b)   The size of crew.

c)   The times of filming, for example 12-hour days, as well as the time of day – day, night or unsociable hours.

d)   Whether they would have their own caterers or rely on us.

e)   The cost per day or part of day.

f)   Details of contracts and method of payment, including the length of time – money might be left on deposit.

g)   Which rooms or areas of the estate would be required for filming. What would the requirements be for artistes, make-up, hairdressers and extras. All of this had to be settled before the crew arrived.

h)   Requirements regarding fires and smoke guns. Smoke guns could only be used with the permission of the owner as valuable items such as paintings, textiles and marble could be damaged by smoke. If permission was granted, the fire alarm company had to be alerted so that sections of the alarms could be taken off for a limited period during filming. Fire alarms had to be fully operational again before film crews departed.

i)   Any rooms not required for filming were locked for security purposes. Furniture not required was to be stored to prevent damage.

j)   Prior to the main film crew arriving on site, props were delivered and stored and the set erected.

k)   Parking areas were required for film crew staff and the catering van. Signs had to be put up. Access to power supply was required unless the crew brought its own generators. Toilet facilities had to be arranged. Vans often contained hairdressers, artistes, make-up, lighting, cameras, directors and producers.

l)   Before anyone set foot on the premises on the first day, the floors had to be covered. Staff and security were issued with radios and given their positions. All signs for the premises were erected, ashtrays and bins positioned outside and an area for tea/coffee breaks allocated.

m)   No smoking, no food (except during designated breaks) and no sitting on the furniture was allowed at any time.

n)   Security was vital and was operational as soon as everyone arrived outside. Radios, too, were very important.

o)   Agreement on outside security should have been reached.

p)   Staff as well as security had to be vigilant at all times. All small items, books or anything easily stolen were locked away and brought out again if required during filming. Trust had to be earned and crews respected this. Firmness regarding where the crew might or might not go was essential. So was awareness of the owner's property and potential damage to items inside and out. Crews tended to leave things leaning on walls without protection. To prevent damage to carpets they were taken up, covered with dust-sheets and the joins taped or essex-boarded on top. The same applied to any polished floors. The owner's furniture was not to be moved without consulting staff or security. Furniture was only allowed to be moved by the film crew if staff or security were present and permission granted.

q)   Most crews were manageable and respected their environment. Consideration was given to the fact that they can get bored standing around, especially during set-ups and filming itself. This was when security was very important too.

r)   A sweep of all rooms each evening after film crews departed was made in order to check for any damage (which was noted and reported). Any cable obstructing windows which needed to be closed was disconnected and laid neatly on the floor. Disconnection of cables usually occurred before crews departed but was sometimes forgotten.

s)   Film crews usually appointed someone to empty rubbish, clean the toilets and make sure things were tidy. Any damage was assessed on the final day and reported to the owner and the film crew's agent, together with details of any items missing.

t)   It was very important to find out who was who and adjust the staff and security accordingly, giving everyone a brief and a script each day and an idea of the rooms being used.

u) The main stars, directors and producers needed to be treated with tact and diplomacy according to their importance. (Having said that, everyone on a film crew feels pretty important!) All crew and anyone concerned with the filming had to know who was who in the owner's team of staff and security. Someone was allocated to the room where filming was taking place and someone else instructed to give them a break after a few hours. During breaks, lunch and dinner the owner's staff had to be around and take their breaks at a convenient time. Security needed to be extra vigilant as this was the time things went missing. Everyone had to be alert at all times.

v) Stars are very important people so if autographs were required there had to be a set procedure in place. The location manager needed to be consulted.

FILMS AND FILM SHOOTS WHICH HAVE TAKEN PLACE AT HIGHCLERE

1986   *The Secret Garden*
1987   *Poor Little Rich Girl*
       Blott on the Landscape
1988   *Mystery of the Pyramids Live*
1989   *The Free Frenchman*
       The Secret Life of Ian Fleming
1990   *The Prince of Crime: Sherlock Holmes* (English version)
       (*Hands of a Murderer* was the American version)
1990   *Duel of Hearts*
       The Grand Piano Came by Camel
       King Ralph 1
       Jeeves and Wooster
       Parts of *Robin Hood Prince of Thieves*
1991   Fosters Beer commercial
       Jeeves and Wooster
1992   *A Sense of History*
       In the Face of Tutankhamen
       BBC *Trainer*

Hunt Clothes commercial
Travel Programme for Middle East Broadcasting
Jeeves and Wooster
1993   *The Pier*
        Stick With Me Kids
1994   BBC *Top Gear*
1995   Volkswagen advertisement
1996   BBC *The Road Show*
        BBC Schools Programme – *Writing and Pictures – The Story Store*
        Ridge-Ridges
        Rover Car Advertisement
        Nissan Car Advertisement
1998   *Great House Game*
        Great Garden Game
1999   *Return to the Valley of the Kings*
        Trade Secrets
        Nestle *Mega Truffle* Ice Cream Advertisement
        Volkswagen Cars Advertisement
        Red Label Tea Advertisement for Canadian Television
        Mini Mars Advertisement
        Antiques Roadshow
        High Stakes at Highclere

My radio and TV appearances

Trade Secrets on BBC2 was a programme where I had to demonstrate housekeeper's tips, like cleaning teapots and how to get rid of water stains and dog hairs. Nearly 200 tips were given on the programme and some of them were included in a BBC book, also called *Trade Secrets*.

High Stakes at Highclere was filmed over a period of a year and portrayed life at Highclere both inside the house and on the estate, focusing on the family and their racing circle. I was filmed doing household duties, attending the worst function at Highclere – computer people from Basingstoke – talking to the Carnarvons and being present at the arrival of the new Castle manager. This programme was on Channel 4.

The Great House Game involved two couples competing to find the best artistic pair. Lord and Lady Carnarvon were supposed to preside over the game but Lord Carnarvon was ill in London so Lady Carnarvon was unable to attend. The Castle manager was at Towcester attending a race meeting with his faithful friend Ashley in the Bentley. On being asked who would do the programme, he said: "You. I'm only at the other end of the phone, so give me a shout if you need anything". With that he left me to get on with it. Well, this was probably the worst day of my life. Fortunately I got through it with the help of my friend Diana. She took me through the State Rooms with Eric Knowles, who was showing people the house once the competition had started. The couples had to rethink two screens and match them to the décor in the Castle; one was a bedroom and the other the dining room. I had to judge them. It was certainly different, I'll say that.

Eric Knowles talked knowledgeably about various pieces of furniture, Egyptian artefacts and china. He also talked about the history of the Castle and the Carnarvon family. Apparently, on returning from his meeting, Adrian Wiley said he had every confidence in me; it would have helped if he'd told me that beforehand! Actually, all I really lacked was self-confidence because I knew I had this awful habit of saying the wrong thing and putting my foot in it.

BBC *Radio 5 Live* – I was asked to give a talk at the local radio station in Newbury on clocks at Highclere Castle. Off I trotted as this didn't seem too difficult. I was escorted into a small room in the Newbury Council Offices and then into a cubicle. Laugh? I was in stitches. On the way there I'd been telling myself how I'd talk to the interviewer, underlining my points with various hand gestures, but now there was just a cubicle and a microphone. I laughed so much at my naivete that the talk came easily, like chatting to my best friend. On the way home I was still laughing about the whole episode. I did a few more interviews for radio on handy tips at the Castle and, as time went by, it became easier and easier.

Allerton Castle, Yorkshire, before it was burnt to the ground in 1999

John Hurt, filmed at Highclere

Tom Cruise and Nicole Kidman
©Alan Davidson/The Picture Library Ltd.

Marco Pierre White
©Alan Davidson/The Picture Library Ltd.

Team building - 'Skipper Mo'

Frozen Highclere

Motivator winning the 2005 Vodafone Derby
Picture courtesy of Highclere Thoroughbred Racing Limited

Adrian shooting

Dusky

Wedding ceremonies and receptions held at Highclere Castle

The first wedding reception during my time at Highclere was actually Lady Carolyn Herbert's, when the 6th Earl was alive, although it was in a marquee on the east lawn outside the Library. Part of the house was open as the 6th Earl was in residence. This occasion saw Sarah & Mary Catering at Highclere for the first time. Lady Carolyn Herbert married Mr John Warren (whose father lived on a council estate) on 20th July 1985. Prince Andrew and Lady Diana attended and most of the estate came to greet them on their return from the church but were told to keep their distance by Robert the butler. The marquee was used for farm manager Harold Vine's retirement party. I helped Sarah and Mary for nothing in the catering marquee so that I could be part of the proceedings as Robert didn't want too many people around in the Castle.

Geordie Porchester's wedding reception following his marriage to Jayne Wilby took place on Saturday 16th December 1989 at Highclere. The saloon benefited from a new carpet bought for the occasion. The Queen and Princess Margaret attended – Geordie is one of The Queen's godsons. Jane later produced a daughter (Saoirse) and a son (George) who is the heir and will be the 9th Earl of Carnarvon one day.

The Hon. Harry Herbert married Chica at Highclere Church and they had their reception at Highclere Castle on Saturday 19th December 1992. I organized the staffing for drinks and canapés for over 400 guests. Princess Diana and The Queen attended. At that time there was a great deal in the press suggesting that The Queen and Princess Diana had fallen out and were barely speaking. However they greeted each other with genuine affection and spent time with each other.

The 7th Earl would not allow wedding receptions at Highclere. However, he agreed, as a wedding gift, to let two long-standing members of his staff, namely Martin Giles and Lindsey Hardham, hold their reception within the Castle. There were no further wedding receptions until Adrian Wiley became Castle manager. Adrian suggested to the 7th Earl of Carnarvon that the Castle should become registered for civil marriage ceremonies and our first wedding was that of Beverley Whent, whose father was the managing director of Vodafone. The couple have since divorced.

One wedding with a difference was that of Rita Spaventa and Preston Fairfax Jr. There were no guests, so staff at the Castle were asked to be witnesses and guests as well. The wedding took place on the 4th July 2000 and the ceremony was conducted by the Reverend Quentin Gelder. I have vivid memories of the Reverend playing croquet on the Castle lawns with his cassock tucked between his legs. Paul Hodges, our resident Castle artist, was asked to give a reading and when he got up to do this he realised he'd mislaid his glasses. I was drafted in to be a witness. Rita was dressed in a stunning fairytale dress like Cinderella. Preston Fairfax Jr looked just like Fred Astaire, dressed in top hat and tails and carrying a walking stick. Six of us joined the bride and groom and dined with them in style in the State Dining Room. The couple had asked if there were any casinos near Highclere and following the meal we all went by taxi to one in Reading. What a stir Rita caused when she went in – she was still wearing her wedding dress! The players in the casino, many of them Chinese, couldn't believe their eyes and everyone stopped what they were doing and looked on in amazement. The manager came over to greet us. He would have offered the bride and groom champagne, but it was late on a Sunday and the licensing laws prevented it.

Another unusual wedding took place between a long net man and a goat lady who were members of the Southern Counties Fair team which came to Highclere every year. When they arrived on the morning of their event for a rehearsal they had no bridesmaid, so guess who had to take over? Me! Mr & Mrs Brindley had their ceremony in the saloon. I wore a dress and jacket and the guests from the Southern Counties Fair came just as they were – wellies, plus fours etc. The music they requested was *Run Rabbit Run* and *The Floral Dance*. *The Archers* theme tune was chosen for the wedding. It was really hilarious, and had all been arranged by Adrian and the Scutt brothers (Tony and Roger), who owned and ran the Southern Counties Fair. Unfortunately, the marriage did not last very long.

I remember one bride had no wedding nerves at all until we walked through the drawing room and music room. Awaiting the cue to go through the Library door for the ceremony to commence she suddenly froze and said she couldn't go through. Adrian was saying to me on the radio: 'Maureen, we're ready' and still she wouldn't go. I quickly gave her a squeeze of the hand and pushed her through the door. Once she saw everyone she automatically proceeded down the aisle without a second thought. She wrote and thanked me when she was in Australia – without me she wouldn't have taken that vital step. All in a day's work!

Diana Moyse, formerly a guide and then a housekeeper, found a girl fast asleep during a wedding in East Anglia bedroom; she'd had a lot to drink and was just sleeping it off.

GREG RUSEDSKI AND LUCY CONNOR'S WEDDING

From the first time that I met Lucy and her mother Margaret and Aunt Kathy, I knew that the wedding breakfast would take place at Highclere. Lucy's face lit up when I opened the front door. There was such warmth and enthusiasm there. At the time I wasn't aware that her fiancé was Greg Rusedski and in any case I'd never heard of him. The rapport was so strong that even I was getting excited and suggested to Lucy that, on the morning of her wedding, she should go and play tennis or golf. Her prompt answer was: "How did you know that my fiance is a tennis star?" I didn't. We laughed and instantly she was on her mobile to America, talking to Greg and telling him this was the venue where they'd be having their wedding breakfast. Lucy fell in love with the magic of Highclere and its surroundings. Her aunt was my parents, solicitor – what a small world it is.

Greg Rusedski was with Lucy the next time they came. He didn't want any members of the public to be there, which I found odd, because it was the public who loved him. You can find fame and fortune through sheer hard work, but without the support of the public you're nothing. As the ladies of the Connor family went about exploring and making decisions, he sat down in the saloon. Curiosity got the better of me. As I'd been introduced on their arrival I thought I'd see what this Greg was all about. Well, to my surprise he was like a giant, of very masculine build but also very gentle. He asked me to sit down and keep him company, thinking no doubt that they'd let him know when a decision was required. We talked about different things and he asked me if I knew anything about tennis. Not a thing, I replied. I hadn't realized how famous he was but he was delightful and on his departure he gave me a kiss on the cheek, as the rest of the family did. They were off to Douai Abbey to make arrangements for the ceremony.

WEDDINGS FROM A HOUSEKEEPER'S POINT OF VIEW

Preparations for a wedding were sometimes a little hair-raising, especially when a helicopter was bringing guests or the groom. Maureen was out there like a shot (to assist, of course). Wedding days were long, especially during our public opening season, but they were very rewarding because no two of them were ever the same.

Quite often it was my duty to build a special relationship with the bride and the bride's mother – something I loved because every wedding was special. It was their very special day and they needed to relax and enjoy it. I was there to create a relaxed atmosphere and take all the tension away. A few kind words would put them at ease and, to calm them still further, a bottle of champagne or a gin and tonic, maybe even a good old-fashioned brew-up, would help enormously. If none of these things worked then the last resort was my herbal remedy. Many mothers had good intentions but sometimes their presence created more tension and made the bride more nervous. At each wedding you could always be sure that someone would need my expertise – a bow tie tweaked or tied, buttons to be sewn on, stains to be taken out of clothes, taxis ordered, soles to be stuck on shoes. Guests would sometimes arrive early and need to be looked after.

The atmosphere at some weddings was electrifying because, after the ceremony, people relaxed and the celebrations began. However, only after the speeches did the party commence. There were some really jolly times. One chap suddenly whisked me on to the dance floor. Apparently it was an impulse as he'd never done anything so daring. It was wonderful and I could have danced all night.

We had some beautiful weddings, including the one where the bride was dressed in black with white trimmings and insisted that rows and rows of chairs should be put out for the ceremony. We had Indian, Hindu, Jewish and Japanese guests, and there was the time Hello! magazine came to cover the wedding of Liza Minelli's daughter. All were full of glamour, richness and colour, providing wonderful memories.

We were often exhausted by 1.30am but would set to and put all the furniture back, ready for cleaning a few hours later. Then we'd sit down for a well-earned drink and I'd put my trainers on, which was a must – if I summoned up the energy, that is.

Initially weddings caused us problems but then, of course, we became more experienced and learned about problem areas. These may be summarised as follows.

Flowers draped across the fireplaces: They looked very pretty but became top heavy and toppled over with flower water going everywhere. Even when the florist, who came from Marlborough, assured everyone it couldn't possibly happen because she'd done it so many times before, it still did. Consequently she and her team were banned from our florists, list.

Flowers raised above the saloon: Suspended by ropes and tied to the balustrades. Care had to be taken to protect the stonework, with a watchful eye kept on the florist. Not ideal.

Flowers on the banisters: When I'd polished the staircase thoroughly, the florist would sometimes tell me that flowers would be draped over the banisters. This nearly gave me heart failure, but great care was taken and the wood protected. Some florists were very sympathetic and went about their work with great respect for the beautiful things around them. Such a display looked wonderful and was allowed on certain occasions.

Candles in floral arrangements freestanding on the marble floor: There was the time the 'non-drip' candles dripped over the marble. No one had allowed for the front door being opened and closed, with the draught causing a big problem.

Rose petals and confetti: Banned after a while because they were trodden in everywhere and ended up in the unlikeliest places, causing particular problems when wet. Across the lawns was the best place for them.

The majority of **guests** showed great respect for their surroundings but some were sick over the carpets or in the bathrooms, because they couldn't hold their drink. This was the unpleasant part of the job.

We had to protect the polished wooden floors from bands sticking **gaffa tape** down instead of using rubber tracking to tidy their wires.

Throughout a wedding the **photographers** had to be watched very carefully. If our resident photographer, Richard Summersby, was on duty things went very well. When it rained he would quite often need my assistance to hold an umbrella over the bride (the groom was fine) until the photograph was taken. He was so good. But other photographers did entirely their own thing and sometimes took liberties. We had to be careful when furniture was moved for family photos. Some photographers stood on the furniture or stonework or suddenly, just when dinner was imminent, whisked the bride and groom away for more photos leaving guests waiting for the meal to be served. On one occasion the toastmasters came to Highclere Castle to familiarise themselves with the wedding venue. After lunch they asked for their photographs to be taken. Chris Marfleet obliged, which was greatly to his credit because he was very busy at the time and I felt a bit sorry for him. There were some magnificent poses but, when they left, he discovered there was no film in his camera. He was devastated and we didn't know how to tell Brian Sylvester and his friends, but Chris did in the end. It was just a genuine mistake.

Bands or discos had to be escorted into the saloon and kept an eye on as many thought they could do just as they liked, although others respected their surroundings. They would position lights over the balustrades, chipping the walls or paintwork – everything had to be monitored.

In the saloon, when there was Ceilidh dancing, we had to be careful as they made the four light clusters vibrate and my staff or someone else had to keep hold of them.

Cakes were often displayed on the staircase near the statue or in one of the fireplaces in the Library, depending on the number of guests. Only once have I seen a cake, leaning like the Tower of Pisa, fail to stay straight. It was because the icing was too soft, but the base of a baking cake tin did the trick until the photographs had been taken.

On odd occasions we'd find cake or other bits of food tucked under the stair carpet, in vases, drawers, even down toilets. You can't prevent that.

LINDSEY AND MARTIN'S WEDDING

On the day Lindsey (who worked for The Hon. Harry Herbert, then managing the Castle) was to be married to Martin Giles (Martin had been responsible for the forestry on the Carnarvon estate for 20 years), she had taken a booking for a Peugeot Family Fun Day event to take place within Castle Piece, a field opposite the Castle. This was on the understanding that the client did not need to use the Castle itself and therefore the event would not impinge on her wedding reception inside. At this point she did not know that the client also needed the area directly outside the front door! I know Lindsey could have told the client that the date was unavailable, but she thought it only fair to accept a booking that would make money for the Carnarvons whereas her own wedding would not, because the reception was a gift from the family.

However, this Peugeot event was not a good thing from anyone's point of view, especially mine, as it nearly got me the sack! The week before the happy occasion John Mason was putting plenty of effort into cleaning his tractor and trailer. Whenever the opportunity arose, he would tease Lindsey and say that he was getting it ready for the wedding. Unknown to both of them we were using a car, although so far we hadn't worked out how we were going to get them to the front door of the Castle. A plan would be devised, no doubt.

We had permission to take the wedding couple via the back route past the kitchen, depositing them at the rear door right at the back (Jack Day's door to us), or go up the steps and walk them to the front door. These were the only options. Blow that for a lark! By hook or by crook they'd be driven to the front door and enter the proper way, or my name wasn't Maureen Cummins. I told all this to John Mason, who was organising the transport. He just winked at me and said: "Leave it to me, Mo". Everything was organised inside the Castle by me and the rest of the team and on the day all we had to do was wait for the OK by radio when they left the church. Over the radio came John's voice: "Approaching the crossroads, will be there in a few minutes". But the next minute he came through the gates, right in the middle of traffic and in full view of everyone, and drove straight up to the front door. I asked him how he'd managedit. "I just followed everyone else. There was a sign at the crossroads but I forgot to tell everyone I can't read", he winked at me. Then he took the car into the courtyard. Mission accomplished. We'd set out to give Lindsey and Martin a proper arrival and it was great. However, unbeknownst to me the person in charge of the other event had gone storming off to Harry in the office and made a formal complaint. What a miserable old bag she was; she'd also given me a great deal of verbal abuse beforehand. I was in deep, deep trouble, believe me.

The next day I was ordered to see Harry in his office. He said: "We've had a complaint from Peugeot about you. Apparently you went against all their wishes and took Lindsey and Martin to the front door and caused an uproar". I explained that it wasn't intentional but a spur of the moment decision. John couldn't read the sign so he thought it best to go with the flow of cars and had unfortunately swerved left to avoid a collision. At that point he thought it best to drop the pair of them at the front door. Mr Harry said: "You realise you could be sacked for this".

Oh! Quite right, I said, but they both had a wonderful day and were overjoyed at coming through the front door on their wedding day. I got a right ticking off but he thought it was unintentional and told me to be careful how I spoke to people if a similar situation arose again. I can't remember the name of the event organiser but everything had worked out the way we wanted, thanks to John. Apparently Lindsey was very relieved when it was a car that arrived to take them to the reception and not the dreaded, decorated tractor and trailer.

My love of fine wines

It was during Robert Taylor's time at Highclere that my interest in fine wines took hold. I rarely tasted them, but was intrigued by the 6th and 7th Earl's cellars. I was allowed into them only if Robert went to collect wines for special occasions or shoots. He was the only one who had the keys. After Robert's death, Les Taylor (the security officer) was put in charge of the cellars that were now the 7th Earl's, together with the champagne cellars.

Credit for most of the tastings at Highclere must go to Adrian Wiley. Wine tastings in the cellars were popular with clients and wine agents came to set them up. Wine fairs were exciting and fascinating and the atmosphere was very special. You couldn't taste all the wines at wine fairs. You needed an idea of what you wanted to taste and why, together with an awareness of the food the chef had prepared for a particular season. It was great that Adrian loved wines too. His knowledge was far greater than mine, but he encouraged me and let me store my own collection in the cellars, ranging from Grand Cru Montrachets to fine burgundies and great dessert wines. At commercial wine tastings, weddings, etc., he always said that I was too direct with my comments but usually he could tell what I thought, just by looking at my face.

At Highclere we had some wonderful, affordable wines on our list, particularly a Chilean Chardonnay called Medrano and a splendid Rioja. There were also some exceptional wines served at some of the Highclere weddings. A Japanese wedding had a Haut Brion (1950) but most of it was poured down the sink because they only took a sip out of politeness to their hosts. I remember this particular wedding quite fondly as Adrian and my son Chris had the 'arduous' task of opening and tasting every bottle to ensure that the wine was not corked. At Bob Rae's wedding Chateau Cantemerle was served, and at the Russian – Diggle wedding it was Pouilly Fuisse Grand Cru. If the top-class wines requested were not available, clients were allowed to bring their own and pay corkage. But Highclere's list was very impressive, with the finest wines as well as magnificent vintage ports brought up from the 7th Earl's cellars for events like Marco Pierre White's shoots. All had to be tasted, of course.

Special occasions came along like the St Emilion evenings when dinners consisted of five courses with ten wines. I spent hours engrossed in books, either in the Library or at second hand bookshops reading about different classifications and ceremonies connected with wines, especially the St Emilion Jurade ceremony. But nothing came close to the fine burgundies I'd tasted. A few Pinot Noirs from South Africa might have the edge but personally I love white wines. On a trip to South Africa I found a wonderful wine at the Hamilton Russell vineyards. The Hamilton Russell Chardonnay was exquisite, out of this world. The Hempel Hotel in London organised a dinner where South African wines were served. This was where I discovered the Hamilton Russell Ashbourne, a wine that even Nelson Mandela couldn't get hold of. The Pinot Noir was as outstanding as I could possibly have imagined. If I could afford it this would be my chosen wine, next to the burgundies.

During a relaxing holiday in Madeira I was privileged to be shown around the vineyards and cellars of Henriques et Henriques where my friend and I were given a full demonstration of the techniques involved in making this fine fortified wine. I fell in love with it and long for the day when it regains its rightful place in the British market place. People associate Madeira with after-dinner drinking but it can also be enjoyed as an aperitif. A whole meal can be created around the four different styles of Madeira and it is a great pity that it seems to have fallen out of fashion.

14TH FEBRUARY 1997 – MY SON CHRISTOPHER'S 20TH BIRTHDAY AND THE OPENING OF THE GRAND CRU LA MONTRACHET 1990 – QUEEN OF THE BURGUNDIES

As we approached Day's Cottage at 8pm, my husband Tony remarked: "No babysitter's car. Something's amiss, has the evening been cancelled?"

"Oh, no!" I said. "Adrian has something up his sleeve, don't worry". On entering the cottage I noticed Tony's eyes drifting left – he'd seen the table set for a meal, and realised something was afoot. There was a warm and friendly atmosphere as we arrived, generated by Adrian and Mary, our hosts for the evening, who wished Chris a happy birthday. Moet & Chandon champagne was served, with apple juice for Tony. Adrian explained the circumstances; owing to its being St.Valentine's evening no tables or babysitters were available so he would act as chef at home.

At last the moment arrived and we sat down to dinner. Foie gras was presented with a 1995 Baron Rothschild Sauterne, the delicate sweetness balancing the rich pate. The second course consisted of baked tomatoes with balsamic vinegar, chopped garlic and basil along with the Louis Latour 1994 Grand Montagny 1er Cru. Again, food and wine complemented each other perfectly. The colour and taste of the wine were wonderful compared to other Montagnys that I'd tried. Conversation flowed and there was keen anticipation as the time approached for the next wine to be served. The La Montrachet had been decanted. It looked young in colour but the flavour was smooth – bouquet and taste in perfect harmony. These were sublime moments made possible by everything that a wonderful wine can offer.

The main course consisted of roast lamb with seasonal vegetables and roast potatoes, accompanied by a Chateau Batailley Grand Cru 1966. This was a Pauillac of considerable distinction, full of flavour and every bit as special as the La Montrachet. We drank it with total enjoyment – what a wine. I could slip into this way of life with no trouble at all! As the meal progressed the wines were the main topic of conversation. To appreciate fully the La Montrachet we went back to taste the Montagny. What a contrast: it now tasted like nothing on earth! If I were to try to explain, it tasted bitter and unpalatable, nothing like the beautiful flavour we experienced when dinner began. The Montrachet would win without a doubt.

Individual fruit tartlets with kiwi and lychees were beautifully presented and much enjoyed. What a meal – the table, the company, the fine wines – all came together to make this an enchanting evening. All that remained was to do justice to the well-matured brie.

Time was passing so enjoyably, we'd had a fantastic evening, and then suddenly the vintage port appeared – Taylors 1985, how wonderful. A rare Hennessy cognac rounded things off. Oh my goodness, how spoilt we'd all been and what marvellous hosts we'd had. Adrian had given us a truly memorable time on this glorious day and it will never be forgotten. There had been a worrying moment or two when Tony didn't realise where he was going for the evening or what he was eating. But thank you, Adrian and Mary, for making Christopher's 20th birthday a day neither he nor I will ever forget.

The Montrachet and Pauillac heightened my desire to learn more about the best food and drink the world has to offer. My education had just begun and Chris and I benefited from Adrian's knowledge. The Queen of Burgundies came up to my highest expectations and I am looking forward to drinking the next few bottles. What precious memories.

FRIDAY 25TH JUNE 1999 – THE GERALD BENNEY WINE CHALLENGE
The idea of a wine challenge came about over dinner one evening, when the general preference seemed to be for French wines over Australian. The cry went up for a wine challenge, with each couple having to name their country of choice and bring along representative wines for each course. I had agreed to help by serving them. The day arrived, preparations began, silver was cleaned

and there were fifty glasses for each course. Each course was to be taken in a separate room. Janet Benney had this brilliant idea and the challenge took place at the Benneys, house in Cholderton. The dress code was black tie and everyone arrived appropriately dressed and in a jolly mood.

Guest list: Professor Gerald and Janet Benney
               Sir David and Lady Lucy Brooke
               Adrian and Mary Wiley
               James and Noel O,Brien
               Bob and Fiona Rae

This was going to be a fun evening but where the wines were concerned everyone was deadly serious. The evening was young. James, the Australian supporter, was early with his wines and decanted his red into one of Gerald's huge glass decanters. He seemed to think he was ahead of the others. The grin on James's face was mischievous, shall we say. Unknown to all of them I had decided to pour the wines before they went for each course to stop any cheating.

The Wiley camp seemed to have a trump card up their sleeve, their wines being from South Africa. His red had been opened a few hours earlier and his white had apparently been taken care of throughout the journey. But his dessert wine presented a problem because there was no known appropriate wine on the market in Great Britain. Apparently, the wine had come straight from South Africa, though this seemed highly unlikely to the best of our knowledge. Time would tell.

Gerald had a twinkle in his eye and was acting like a little boy, but wouldn't say what his dessert wine was. He had chosen the French wines. We were to find out later why he was acting that way. I was distracted by James, who was up to something again. I could see I'd have my hands full later on. The Brooke contenders had chosen wines from Italy and handed them over without any fuss. Now there was only the Rae family to come and their wines were from California. Surprisingly enough, Bob seemed very confident that he would win.

The reception drinks were served – Vodka Pimms and bowls of nibbles – this taking place around the floodlit swimming pool within the glorious surroundings of the Benney garden. The evening was young and full of exciting things to come. Laughter echoed around the garden. Meanwhile, last-minute preparations were being made. The kitchen was alive with action as final arrangements for dinner were made. The dogs trooped in nuzzling my hand. Rastus the Great Dane raised his head as if to ask why I was here. Tenderly I stroked his head and sent him off to bed. The creamer was full to the brim with white wines. The heady aroma of venison drifted around. The kitchen had to be sorted out because it was mayhem in there and resembled a battlefield. Fires in the rooms had to be attended to while the cook was putting the finishing touches to the meal. They were to start with prawns in a mayonnaise sauce and Bloody Mary mousse appropriately garnished.

It was time for the guests to be seated in the drawing room and the challenge to begin. The first wines were poured:

France –   Puligny Montrachet 1993
South Africa –   Hamilton Russell Ashbourne 1996
Australia –   Petaluma (Piccadilly Valley) 1996
Italy –   Terri de Brognoligo 1997
California –   Shafer Chardonnay 1997

As they all entered, the crackling fire enhanced the glorious surroundings. Squeals of delight and anticipation drifted around the room. Before taking their places they all wished each other the best of luck. This was the start of an exciting evening. The food was served, the wines cautiously sniffed, tasted and comments noted. The final choice was made and the Ashbourne won hands down: 9-1 to South Africa. Discussions continued and more wine was taken. Meanwhile the second course was prepared and the wines poured. These were:

France –	Haut Brion 1986
South Africa –	Hamilton Russell Pinot Noir 1997
Australia –	Tim Adams, The Aberfeldy 1997
Italy –	Brunello in Paradiso 1993
California –	Morgan Pinot Noir

Guests were asked to withdraw from the drawing room and take their places in the dining room. I could see a little cheating was going on. Certainly they were all entering into the spirit of things and I suspected it was something James had done that prompted roars of laughter.

In this genial mood the main course was served – Highclere roebuck with all the trimmings. It looked so succulent, oozing with blood and a beautiful rich sauce. By now I was fairly certain about the cheating but, unbeknownst to them, I'd changed the colour coding so this baffled them all – clever rascals, or so they thought. Time to go and sort them out. Laughter still echoed down the passageway as I approached – they were certainly up to no good. France, California and Australia drew 3-all, but suddenly there was a shout from Bob Rae. "Hey James, I thought you'd chosen purple as your first choice, not green?" James had swapped the colour codes again. In fact it wasn't a draw because the Californian wine, Morgan Pinot Noir, had won by a single vote. Just as well I'd changed the codes for dessert, because I knew I'd have trouble with James and Adrian. Gerald's Haut Brion would have been my own choice as I am very fond of French wines.

Taking a few minutes to relax, I suddenly sensed there was someone in the drawing room with me. It was dear Gerald; they'd all persuaded him to open another bottle so they were happy for a while. He seemed very relaxed too and chatted amiably. I got on so well with him and he was really enjoying himself, he kept smiling all the time. But I wonder! Something told me he was up to something. Walking out of the room and entering the kitchen I noticed he'd decanted his dessert wine. This was unusual to say the least, but I knew he had an ace up his sleeve and something underhand was going on. Huge bets had now been placed so things were getting serious.

The laughter had stopped and discussions were in progress. Now that everyone was back in the dining room I could return to the drawing room and pour the dessert wines. Tasting Gerald's wine I found it very good indeed. It was stunning. I wasn't really up on dessert wines but there was something about this one that convinced me something was happening. But what? Everyone gathered back in the drawing room, the fire was blazing away and the table was set for dessert. The wines were approached tentatively and for some reason everyone had mellowed a great deal. Whatever had taken place next door there was mischief afoot and Gerald had a smile like a Cheshire cat; he'd never make a good poker player. Everyone went quiet suddenly. Either they were all being polite to their hosts or they thought it was an excellent wine. Amazingly it was 9-1 to the French, even though the South African runner-up was better by far. But what was the mystery? There was definitely something going on. After a few more discussions Gerald won the bet and took charge of the winnings. Now we would find out what the wine was. It certainly complemented the poached peaches marinated in brandy and banoffee pie.

Cheese was available but everyone was tucking into the wonderful dessert. As I was preparing coffee to take out to the garden the mystery was solved. Apparently it wasn't a French wine but Mrs Littlewood's elderflower wine from the village. What a hoot! An absolute classic. The guests withdrew to the gardens draped in shawls and blankets as the night chill crept in. Armagnac and port were offered and went down well. The bottles from the dinner were put out on display. Then I left them to it and went to help cook clear up and relax a little. They'd all be in shortly as the night air seemed unusually crisp. Half an hour later I heard laughter from the music room; songs were being sung by the piano and some of the guests were chattering in the hallway. This continued for quite a while and the Cholderton Wine Challenge drew to an end. The Ashbourne certainly won hands down, the Morgan took the main course and, as far as the dessert wine was concerned, Gerald's homemade challenger certainly triumphed!

Who will attend the next wine challenge? I don't know. "I naturally assume that the chinaman will not be present at the next wine challenge?" said David Brooke. Luckily Bob Rae, who was of Chinese extraction, had already departed. It was marvellous that people could enjoy themselves and have such fun, all because of a challenge. I certainly enjoyed myself and had a wonderful evening. I was thanked by everyone before they left. 'We're all looking forward to next year!' were the words as they departed.

My parents

During my time at Highclere my parents moved from Co Durham (they retired there) to Hurstbourne Tarrant near Andover. They both suffered from declining health; my mother was disabled and my father had pneumoconiosis (dust on the lungs) from his early years down the pit. I bought a bungalow for them to live in, which was a cash deal except that I was £15,000 short of the asking price. I borrowed the remainder of the money from Johnny Collins. Johnny was Ivy the cook's brother. I worked for her in my earlier years and they both lived in White Oak bungalow near the cricket pitch on the estate when Ivy retired from the Castle. They were both dear friends and Johnny was sorely missed on the estate as he was always good for a laugh. When he worked in the garden shop he had a very special way with the ladies and Jane, Lady Porchester, the 8th Earl's first wife, got on famously with him. The Porchester family lived on the estate at the time.

Every waking minute I took on more work to repay Johnny until my parents, house in the north was sold. He told me that I was an honourable person and he knew I wouldn't let him down. I eventually paid back every penny. It wasn't until I went to South Africa for a holiday in my late forties that I had a bank account. I'd never needed one in the past and kept everything I earned in a cardboard box under the bed. When I bought the house the solicitors were astonished when I walked in with a box filled with £58,000 in cash.

My parents spent the rest of their days at Hurstbourne Tarrant until they died in 1996. My father died in March in the bathroom and was found by the home help carers. I loved him very deeply and losing him was a huge loss to me. I now had to cope with my mother as well as everything else, and she was bedridden. She died in December, I think of a broken heart. I never said goodbye to her and I've regretted it ever since, even though she certainly didn't love me. It took me a long time to overcome my guilt, but I carried out their last wish, which was to have their ashes scattered at sea at Seaham, Co Durham. My friend Diana came with me.

It took me eight years to sell the bungalow. It was extremely hard coming to terms with anything after the events of that year, especially when my eldest brother assumed he'd inherited the bungalow, by virtue of his age. That was when I found out he was my half-brother and he discovered I owned the bungalow. I haven't heard from him since. My sister Margaret stood by me because she was aware of the situation regarding Michael long before I was.

Memories of nature and phenomena at Highclere

I am very privileged to have experienced some marvellous things during my long stay at Highclere; golden moments like the time I saw a magnificent stag on the south lawn and I was rooted to the spot afraid that if I moved or blinked it would vanish. I was unsure of my next move if it charged, although fear never entered my head. It was just a private moment in time and something I may never experience again. I loved to watch deer in beautiful surroundings, nuzzling each other or just peacefully grazing, and there was also the bobbing of the white hare in the field near the field house. It is very rare to see a white hare. As I took my daily walk across the lawns I found a baby owl huddled in the undergrowth, a grey furry bundle squeaking for mother's attention. So many times I've just stood and admired my surroundings with the sun rising and setting. I have many photographs of mist rising with the sun filtering through; different aspects of the seasons at Highclere.

I can recall seeing one of the bulls jump a five bar gate, stride across the road and jump another five bar gate into the next field. Also a vixen and her cubs scampering around the old ice house in Lady Penelope's garden, with the sun beaming down on them. I kicked myself for not having a camera handy but absorbed the moment so that everything was imprinted on my mind forever. I remember a badger scuttling across the tea rooms lawn into the bushes, and someone calling me to the dining room where a long-eared bat had crawled on to the table. It grabbed hold of my finger and was very different from what I'd imagined. The span of its wings was huge and it was very soft.

Many times I would take a walk early in the morning after Tony (my then husband) had gone to work. His attitude was that he was up early so everyone else should be as well. I also had to be at work at 8am. Dawn has always held a fascination for me, especially during the winter months. Whether it's the cold causing me to rub my hands and hunch deep inside my coat, or the trees swaying in the breeze, knowing their remaining leaves will soon be gone forever, the season captivates me. Here are examples of my experiences at these special times.

5th November 1995 7.10am

As I watched the trees droop and shiver in the cold, damp air, I knew that soon their leaves would be discarded with the frost and they'd be left to the cold, unforgiving winds of winter. A couple of deer appeared on the lawn in front of the greenhouses, unaware of my presence. They grazed contentedly, lifting their heads, always alert, watching for the least disturbance. The rays from the sun caught their coats and highlighted their sleekness. As the sun spread itself generously across the land, bringing a bright new day, the glitter of the night frost slowly disappeared. The deer scampered away and the moments of tranquillity were gone. The perfect moment slipped away.

6th November 1995 6.50am

In the distance on the horizon the sun had just awakened, spreading its glow across the dull, shadowy sky. There was the fleeting promise of a wonderful day, but after a few minutes the sun was engulfed by the restless, scudding clouds, leaving the early morning cold with a winter chill in the air.

7th November 1995 6.30am

The chitter-chatter of the birds heralded the dawn, the owl hooted in the distance, lazily aware that night's darkness was evaporating. The pheasants scratched about delightedly, searching for food amongst the foliage and bits of debris.

18th December 1996

The Castle, impervious to the cold, misty morning, stood proud but needed the rays of the sun to warm and brighten the stone, bringing peace and harmony to the mere mortals inside, perhaps. The sun broke through the gloom, creating a soft, beautiful sky. As it dispelled the darkness, forming shafts of flaming red colour among the clouds, the mist drifted and slithered along, creating a blanket of softness below the trees. A gentle breeze picked up the mist, which eddied around the woods, awaiting its fate. The sun gathered together its rays and projected them fiercely on to the stonework of the Castle. Pinnacles stood proudly to attention, like soldiers on parade. A golden glow shot through the windows, enhancing the richness of each and every colour. This would be a wonderful day, full of life, given freely by Mother Nature at her most generous.

The sounds of dawn are rarely heard by the sleepy modern world – the shrill laughter of the blackbirds to say they had seen me, pheasants uttering their clear, early warning as I approached. There was disharmony among the owls when the morning became alive. Traffic rumbled in the distance, the sound of an aeroplane's engines disturbed my tranquil thoughts. A new day dawned.

I recall the joy of awakening to snow, giving me yet another insight into the wonders of nature. The rare sight of the Castle frozen from top to toe, snow and ice having formed on the pinnacles making it look like icing on a cake. All of this brilliance coming together as the night wore on. Arctic scenes as the snow lay undisturbed in drifts two to three feet deep. Cedar limbs broken with the weight suddenly thrust upon them. The lawns covered with snow, not a blade of grass to be seen, but sparkling as the sun's rays caught them. Here was a touch of magic, brought about by something entirely natural. In my 32 years at Highclere, the estate was covered with a blanket of snow on three occasions.

I was very fortunate to experience many of nature's wonders and I have many treasured memories. The winter sun, a few hours after daybreak, was weak and listless, though still prepared to fight the westerly winds tossing dull grey clouds into its path. Spring flowers held their heads up high, seeking the warmth they needed to flourish, but drew back with a sigh, huddling together for comfort against the darkening shadows of the rain clouds. They were waiting and hoping for the wind to blow the rain clouds away, giving the sun's rays a chance to nurture their blooms after a long winter's sleep. Alas, the dull grey clouds engulfed the sky, taking possession of it, and the winter sun withdrew, hoping to fight another day.

Once, as I walked towards Heaven's Gate, watching the sky attentively, a pair of buzzards soared overhead with effortless grace. A cry, that urgent shrill cry of the young, called out to them. They paused briefly to position themselves, waiting for the breeze. Again the cries filled the sky as each thermal carried them closer to their own. These were tranquil moments of freedom, undisturbed by man. The buzzards circled above me, showing off their skills. Reunited with their young, they drifted away gracefully on the breeze, finally disappearing into the distance.

These different scenes are full of the beauty and mystery that only nature can provide, and only we can enjoy – though I shall enjoy them no longer at Highclere.

2nd March 1997
Encouraged by the warm sun, we were inspired one Sunday afternoon to drive out and find some deer. It has always been my dream to photograph deer in magnificent surroundings. Approaching the avenue of trees, my son Chris drove like a daredevil, so keen was he to reach our goal. Twisting and turning along the Grotto Road I shouted to him: "For goodness, sake, slow down!" "Oh Mum, this is great", he replied. "How am I to capture anything on camera if you drive like a lunatic? I need to find the opening to take photographs of the Castle. Slow down! Damn, you've missed it, turn around and go back slowly". "For Christ's sake, mother, who do you think I am?" cried Chris angrily.

We turned the car around and suddenly came face to face with three deer. At first they didn't seem to mind until I wound the window down to take photographs. Camera shy, they bounded through the woods seeking refuge in the dense foliage.

Creeping slowly by Dan's Lodge, we saw them again. They seemed to accept the intrusion and grazed peacefully in the woodlands. Suddenly something seemed to startle them, so they bounded out of sight once more. Hitting and missing the potholes we carried on to Heaven's Gate. It was appropriately named, so beautiful and tranquil, with breathtaking views. It was the closest I'd been to the sky for quite some time. These were moments never to be forgotten and words were inadequate as we made our way slowly back to the car. On the way I spotted more deer. "Stop", I said. Five deer were grazing towards the perimeter of the woods. Slowly and carefully I captured them on film – what a wondrous sight. Kicking my boots off I stood on the seat of the car and popped my head through the sun-roof. Oh, how glorious they were, so graceful and elegant. It is a great pity that they cause such damage to the trees, but nature has a way of looking after its own.

Ron Miles, one of the gamekeepers on the estate, sadly died in 2001. I was unable to attend the funeral. Ron taught me about the deer and each year I would go and sit for many hours, just observing them. Ron would tell me where they were gathering. I took many photographs of them and got very close. They are wonderful creatures and cause no more damage than other things. Human beings cause more damage than anything!

THE GREAT STORM
The year of the great storm in the late 1980s brought an amazing sight. Opening the shutters one January morning, my eyes were confronted by a mass of fallen trees looking towards Siddown Hill. They were like fallen soldiers after a battle; this was nature's way of getting rid of the old and the debris. The previous day, people had been trapped as trees fell across the roads; the

wind caused havoc everywhere. My own worry was how to get my son, Chris, home from school at Burghclere, the next village. I seemed to walk for miles, going through woods from Highclere to Burghclere, because even the main roads were blocked by fallen trees. The sound of chainsaws filled the air, not the sound of traffic. Eventually I arrived at Clere School and walked Chris home safely.

Cedar trees were uprooted throughout the parks of Highclere, falling on to the beautiful lawns surrounding the Castle; craters replacing trees! One of the main cedars in front of the Library, where only the previous December The Queen and the 7th Earl's shooting party had stood, was severely affected by the winds. Lime Avenue on the estate was like a skittle alley as alternate trees crashed to the ground. The whole of the South of England suffered and there was a great sense of loss at Highclere Estate.

Some good did come out of the great storm, however, because Heaven's Gate proudly stood out in all its glory, like a king surveying his land and surroundings. The local paper, the Newbury Weekly News, sent a photographer to record the event.

Maureen's housekeeping tips

- After use in cooking keep lemon halves to rub over hands after scraping carrots or new potatoes. Lemon halves are also good for removing smells from hands.

- Lemons are also great for removing smells and odours from rooms. Smells such as smoke and paint fumes will disappear if you immerse lemons in water and leave them overnight.

- Rub English mustard on chopping boards or hands to remove strong smells such as kippers or haddock.

- If you burn a saucepan, empty the contents out, sprinkle the saucepan with washing soda or salt and cover with water. Bring to the boil and simmer for about 10 minutes. Repeat if necessary.

- If you spill anything on a hot solid fuel cooker, sprinkle salt over the spillage to reduce the smoke and put a few herbs on top of the cooker to take away the smell of burning.

- Sprinkle sea salt on solid fuels to reduce soot.

- A few handfuls of sea salt thrown on to a fire will help reduce smoke.

- A bowl of salt placed in a newly decorated room will get rid of the smell of paint.

- Chew a piece of fresh parsley to get rid of the smell of garlic from your breath.

- A piece of well-washed charcoal in cooking water will reduce the smell from cabbage and onions.

- Adding some milk or a piece of well-washed coal to the water after scraping new potatoes will stop them from going brown.

- Use washing powder or bicarbonate of soda to get rid of tea stains from teapots. Add boiling water, leave to soak then rinse thoroughly.

- Salt moistened on the finger and then rubbed around cups will get rid of stains. Then wash thoroughly. Milton steriliser can be used for teapots or cups in the same way. Soak, then wash thoroughly.

- Put a cube of sugar into a silver or metal teapot before storing it away. This will prevent musty smells.

- Crush an eggshell with a spot of vinegar, put into glass decanters and swirl around to remove port and/or wine stains. Metal shot with vinegar can also be used.

- A splash of vinegar applied to the water when boiling eggs stops them from cracking.

- Get more out of your tube of toothpaste by running the toothbrush handle across the tube.

- When you think you have got to the bottom of the shampoo or soap bottle, take the tops off and add some water.

- When you empty a sauce bottle or pickle jar (not pickled onions) rinse out the jar with a little water and then add to soups, stews and casseroles for extra taste.

- Add a couple of teaspoons of caster sugar to homemade tomato soup to take away the bitterness. A couple of knobs of butter also enriches it.

- To make a crumble crunchier, replace one dessert spoon of flour with one dessert spoon of semolina.

- Rub a used candle on the inside of runners at the back of drawers if they stick. This will loosen them.

- To remove red wine stains from tablecloths, sprinkle on some salt, put the cloth in a bowl so the stain is flat, pour nearly boiling water over the cloth and then launder as soon as possible.

- Also bicarbonate of soda or soda water sprinkled on a red wine stain helps to remove it. Surprisingly, white wine is also an effective way to remove red wine stains from cloth.

- To remove candle wax from a tablecloth, gently lift the wax from the cloth using a knife dipped in boiling water. Sometimes a warm iron and brown paper applied to the wax will also lift it off.

- To stop candles dripping, the ends near the wick should be pared from the wick down. Do this when the candle is cold. In addition, putting a candle in the deep freeze for an hour slows down the burning time.

- Put a little white spirit in a tin of polish and leave it to soak if you have left the lid off and it has dried the polish out.

- To remove NEW liquid stains on wood gently rub dampened cigar or cigarette ash along the grain. Wipe with a damp cloth and then dry and re-polish.

- Dusters will collect dust better if they are ironed after the iron is switched off. This makes them smoother.

- Wash chamois leathers in WARM water, add a drop of ammonia ($\frac{1}{2}$ teaspoon – $\frac{1}{2}$ bowl of water). Use household soap and soak. Squeeze gently to remove dirt. Do not wring. Do this until clean. Squeeze until soft. Then hang to dry naturally. As it dries, rub the sides together to remove the soap and make it soft again.

- A chamois can also be used to bring up the shine on furniture after dusting.

- For any liquid spilt on a carpet, dab it dry with a kitchen towel, apply salt to the area, leave overnight and then hoover. DO NOT RUB THE CARPET as the colours may run.

- To stop windows from steaming up, apply neat washing up liquid or a tiny drop of glycerine.

- Glycerine also stops royal icing from going hard when you are icing a special cake.

- For stamps or envelopes that have lost their adhesive quality, apply the white of an egg then stick down.

- If the top of a bottle, or similar, gets stuck or is too tight, tap its top then run it under the hot tap, this will release it.

- If you run short of cream for patent leather shoes, use Vaseline. Apply a little then rub off with a clean cloth.

- Adding bay leaves to stews, a pot roast or baked rice pudding will give them a nutty flavour.

- Bay leaves are useful for hanging in a wardrobe instead of pot pourri. The leaves deter silver fish. Replace the leaves every 2-3 months.

- Mint finely chopped with caster sugar is a good standby when you run out of mint sauce. Put the cubes in ice trays and freeze.

- Keep all pieces of soap, soak in hot water, then mould together to make a bar for washing hands after gardening and other dirty chores.

- Seal the ends of string, rope and nylon cord to stop them fraying by lighting the ends with a match or lighter.

- Plastic biro cases can be threaded on to light cords to keep them clean.

- If the backs of shoes are rubbing against your heels, rub the inside of the heels with soap or saddle soap.
- Clear nail varnish or clear soap will stop ladders running in tights.

- Clear nail varnish applied to the back of threads stops buttons from coming loose.

- To clean brushes e.g. shoe brushes, clothes brushes, silver brushes, hold a piece of folded wrapping paper around the edge of a table with the rough or dull side facing up. Rub the brushes up and down over the paper.

- Put the handle of a metal spoon into the neck of a champagne bottle to keep the sparkle. When opened, use a cloth to wipe the inside of the bottle to stop it spilling over.

- Wear a pair of rubber gloves dampened with water or dampened hands and wipe over furniture, cloths or car seats to remove pet hair.

- Baking powder or talcum powder applied to the inside of shoes will absorb any smells.

- A squirt from a soda siphon is useful when a pet is sick on the carpet as it gets rid of smells.

- To check if a chimney is clear if you haven't lit it for a while, hold a piece of lighted paper under the inside of the chimney, the smoke will go up if the chimney is clear and down if the chimney is blocked.

- Hold a bottle of wine by the base and flick it if a piece of cork is left in the top after opening it. This will shoot the cork from the bottle.

- Helium balloons held on a piece of string will remove cobwebs from high ceilings.

- Sellotape wound around the hands will remove fluff from trousers after washing.

- Keep a magnet in your sewing box to pick up needles and pins.

- Wine corks on the ends of knitting needles without knobs will prevent the stitches from falling off.

- Knit both sleeves of a cardigan or jumper together to ensure they are identical.

- Put dried teabags sprinkled with methylated spirits around the base of rose bushes to keep greenfly away.

- Refresh tired eyes by putting slices of cucumber on them.

- Spray a candle with perfume to enhance the ambience of your dining room before dinner.

- To clean ivory, brush with soap suds and rinse with lukewarm water. Brush again with a little alcohol. Dry slowly in a gentle heat if yellowish.

- Cover a hoover tool with a nylon stocking and hoover the floor slowly if you have lost an earring or contact lenses.

- To remove sticky labels from glass jars, fill them with hot water so the glue melts from the inside.

- Sometimes, rubbing talcum powder into the edges of floorboards can stop them squeaking.

- To prevent newspapers falling apart use a paper clip.

- Put cling film on to a tabletop to stop residue from plants spoiling the table. This hint can also be used when having a party to stop drink spills.

- Rub the soles of new shoes with sandpaper to take the newness off them.

- Wash tights or stockings all together and put them inside a pillowcase and tie the top. This keeps them from laddering.

- To clean slimy sponges wash in a weak solution of water and vinegar.

- Headaches caused by food or drink can be eased with a hot drink of milk and honey.

- Reduce the smell of garlic by soaking the cloves in cold water an hour before use.

- Always roll an electric blanket to store it or leave it flat on a spare bed.

- Neat vinegar should remove stubborn marks on brick fireplaces, do not use soap or detergent.

- Heavy marble or glass tops should be carried vertically as they can break under their own weight if carried horizontally.

- Store apples stalk down and pears stalk up.

- Hold the lower ends of a pleated shirt with paper clips when packing.

- Brass fittings on wooden furniture can be cleaned with wax polish, brass cleaner leaves a white mark.

- Use a soft pencil on a stuck zip to free it.

- After use, wrap the head of a squeeze mop in a plastic bag to maintain it.

- Run out of face mask? Use whisked egg white.

- A hair dryer can be useful to defrost a fridge or alternatively place a bowl of boiling water inside the freezer and shut the door.

- Fine sandpaper can be used to remove ballpoint pen marks from suede.

- Dip the grater in cold water before grating lemons or oranges, then the peel will slide off easily.

- Clean your liquidizer or food processor by filling half-full with hot water with some washing up liquid and then replace the top and switch on for a few minutes.

- Dab a little lighter fluid on carpets to remove tar. Then wipe off. Then wash with soapy water and dab with a dry cloth.

- Use dried orange or tangerine peel as a means for lighting fires in place of firelighters.

Shoe cleaning

Quite often I was asked as housekeeper to clean shoes, which was a job I loved. In times gone by it was the butler's or valet's job to clean shoes. If your shoes are not clean, then you will not look well dressed. People often scrub shoes to achieve a good deep shine but in fact it's a light quick movement that will give the most wonderful effect.

Nowadays there are many tips for keeping shoes clean but none produces the feeling of deep satisfaction which comes from cleaning a pair of shoes yourself. This is very therapeutic. Years ago and during the early years until the 6th Earl died there was always a boot hall or hole in the house. A good strong table and a deep sink for scrubbing boots and a rack to drain the boots were essential. Many moons ago a footman would never enter if a valet was cleaning shoes or boots. Often people didn't clean the insteps or clean between the stitching under the tongue after loosening the laces. Vinegar was added to blackening to use on shoes and boots. Blackening was put on with a stick and rubbed with a piece of bone. The bone created friction which took out scratches, creating a new surface and a brilliant shine. The best bones for this type of application came from the foreleg of a female deer. The boots and shoes wouldn't take this type of treatment nowadays as the leather would not be thick enough.

A coarse bristle dirt brush should be used to remove dirt from good leather shoes. A very soft bristle for finer leather or even a sponge is recommended to remove dirt. Polish should not be put on to shoes unless dirt is removed first. Shoe cream preserves the leather and keeps it supple, wax polish creates a protective film and makes the leather water-resistant. Saddle soap cleans leather but does not leave much of a shine.

Three brushes should be used to clean shoes:
1) a dirt brush;
2) one to put polish on;
3) soft bristles to take polish off.

Only the dirt brush should be washed and dried naturally. The other two should be cleaned by brushing them on brown paper. The thing to do to achieve a really good shine is to use a very soft duster, which also removes any surplus polish.

Patent leather shoes:- Cream polish or Vaseline can be applied to bring a wonderful shine to this type of shoe. Newer patent leather has a special coating so can be cleaned with a damp cloth.

Suede shoes:- Use a special suede brush to loosen dirt and raise the nap. Brush up the nap, then brush down the nap clockwise. Brushing the whole shoe in the same direction gives a smooth finish.

Nu Buck shoes:- These are usually given a protector spray when new. Clean in the same manner as suede shoes and then apply the protector.

Shoe trees:- Should be used as soon as you take the shoes off, as your shoes will be out of shape and the warmth of your feet will make the leather more pliable. Shoe trees should not be used when the shoe is cold as this will stretch the leather and force it out of shape. Wood and fabric shoe trees are best; wood absorbs the moisture in the leather and fabric allows air to circulate. Damp shoes shouldn't be left, stuff them with newspaper to help the shoes dry before using the shoe trees. Never leave shoes or boots near heat as this will crack the leather. Always keep patent leather shoes wrapped for extra protection.

A few modern tips:

- Wax or furniture polish will give a quick shine when applied and rubbed into shoes with a duster.
- An eraser or baby wipes will clean Nu buck shoes.
- Dyed shoes often mark your feet when wet: spraying the insides of the shoes with scotch guard will stop this.

For boots that you don,t have boot trees for insert empty bottles to make them stand up.

METAL CLEANING

A great deal of elbow grease is called for when cleaning metal but a lot of devotion and passion are involved too. I always use Brasso wadding, not liquid, when I clean metals as I find the liquid dries into nooks and crannies making it hard to clean.

SILVER CLEANING

Silver cleaning is a lost art in the modern world. Many people think that silver cleaning consists of dipping their silver into a silver dip and that's it. Short-term silver can put up with this treatment, but nevertheless it still needs a clean with Goddard's Silver Polish once a year to bring back the shine. Silver or silver plate should not be left in silver dip as doing this removes the plate from the silver.

To clean silver, a piece of baize is necessary to cover the work surface. Items should be properly washed and free from grease. Apply small amounts of silver polish on a cloth or silver brush. When I was first taught by Robert to clean silver he used to use a silversmith's rouge mixed to a creamy consistency then added to one part plate powder with two parts rouge. Plate powder kept the silver from becoming dark and the rouge gave it a deep shine rather than a white look. Rouge contains red oxide of iron; when this was rubbed hard with your finger on the silver it created friction and filled in the scratches. Goddard's Silver Polish was later used in the same way. Soft natural bristle brushes, soft cloths and chamois leathers are needed to complete your cleaning process.

Care should be taken to use different brushes for different jobs. Two long handled ones are required for removing polish from crevices in the silver, the second long handled brush being used to remove traces of polish and bring up the shine. Use flat-backed brushes for larger surfaces and beaded edges, i.e. trays.

Brushes should never be washed. In years gone by whiting was used with newspaper to clean brushes, but today strong white shelf paper wrapped around the edge of a table can be used. Rub the brushes up and down the whole length of the brush until all the residue has been rubbed away.

Sometimes it is necessary to wash silver after cleaning. It is best to do this by hand in hot soapy water if you,ve overused the silver polish. Always wash cutlery and dry thoroughly and polish with a dry duster then a chamois to give the silver an extra shine. Goddard's Silver Polish is brilliant for topping up the shine on silver and buffing with a chamois helps maintain the shine. Obviously, the less you handle silver and leave fingerprints the less it will need polishing. The biggest mistake people make is to apply too much silver cleaning polish and not enough elbow grease, thus making much more work. Small amounts are better.

Silver is a soft metal so it needs careful handling. When storing silver for any length of time it should be wrapped in soft fabric bags or damask napkins and non-acid, strong white tissue paper.

There is a special way to wrap tableware. To wrap it place one piece at a time on its side on the tissue paper a few inches from the edge. Fold the tissue completely over the piece before laying the second piece over the top. At the end you will have a long parcel, tuck in the ends for a good finish. If silver is wrapped properly it can be kept in pristine condition for years.

Removing food stains:- Always wash silver as soon as possible after using it to avoid staining and dried food. Never leave sauce in silver sauceboats or silver spoons in mustard pots or salt cellars. Salt should never be left in silver as it attracts damp. Egg stains silver blue, grouse stains silver all colours and so does anything with garlic in it. Silver dip is excellent for removing these types of stains as well as green stains left by vegetables.

To remove wax:- Never scrape wax from silver candlesticks and never immerse candlesticks in water as this wets the baize on the bottom and causes it to rot. The right way to remove wax is to put the candlestick on a draining board and pour very hot water directly over the candlestick, making sure to angle it to let the water drain and ensure that the baize is kept dry. Remove surface wax, wipe with a damp cloth and then dry with a tea towel before polishing.

COPPER CLEANING

During the days when kitchens were filled with copper pots and pans it was essential to clean the copper and keep it in good condition. The best way to do this was to mix malt vinegar and silver sand into a paste and apply it to the copper. In the past, copper wasn't treated like it is now so it was prone to streaking if not cleaned properly. Brasso is an excellent copper cleaner and you can wipe treated copper with a damp cloth.

PEWTER CLEANING

To make pewter polish years ago you blended equal parts of methylated spirits and whiting together to form a creamy paste which was as thick as double cream. A very small amount was used, rubbed in hard, then the pewter was cleaned with a cloth to bring up the shine. A chamois added a finishing touch. Today, brass and silver polish will produce the same effect.

BRASS CLEANING

Brass should, in theory, be cleaned on a damp day using very little polish or it makes extra work. Embossed parts need to be brushed and an old toothbrush can be used for this. Your breath creates enough moisture to shine brass effectively. However, Brasso and brass cloths can also be used.

Comparisons between rooms and how they were used

There have been quite a few changes since Highclere was a domestic home.

- Wyoming and Vista Rooms were part of Misson's flat and these rooms were bedrooms, bathroom and linen room.

- The studio was a table tennis room.

- The studio store was a dark room where photos were developed.

- The studio kitchen was Robert the butler's bathroom.

- The gents, toilet was the 6th Earl's sauna and toilet (the sauna was originally in the servery).

- The steward's office was Miss Stubbings, office when she was estate manager. After that it was used as the guides, room and later it became my office. When I left, it became a storeroom.

- The 7th Earl of Carnarvon's sitting room was the 6th Earl's study.

- The boudoir was latterly the 6th Earl's bedroom.

- The Carnarvon Room offices were the 6th Earl's master bedroom, ·dressing room and Lady Carnarvon's bedroom.

- Jacky's turret office was a dressing room. It caught fire in the early 70s when a particularly strong sun shone on to a mirror.

- Queen Caroline's Exhibition Room was one of the main bedrooms.

- The passage tea rooms became the 1st staff room.

- The self-service was the 2nd housekeeper's room and laundry room.

- The guides, room – the still room – was used to clean silver and to prepare the early breakfast trays for lady guests. The kitchen was a back scullery with big deep wooden sinks for the preparation of vegetables, making cheeses and homemade ice cream.

- The back entrance was a coal hole to run the coal stove in the kitchen, later converted to accommodate the generator when the coal stove was replaced by a similar stove which ran on oil and electricity. The kitchen was refurbished in 1988, with the stove taken out and replaced by calor gas cookers.

- The kitchen was very Victorian with a large wooden table in the centre and copper and brasses everywhere (mostly used for large parties). Above the range, York hams were cured and hung until needed, especially for shooting parties.

- The room above the kitchens was the cook's office.

- The store near the toilet was the assistant cook's sitting room.

- The tearoom office was the butler's office.

- The children's 'hands-on' room was a boot and brush room, pressing room.

- The wine store was a coal store for the central heating boiler and the fires in the main house.

- The Racing Exhibition was the old servants, hall (previously a nursery).

- The Egyptian Exhibition was the old knife room.

- The display area in the corridor was Jack Day's (electrician's) workshop, previously the oil lamp room.

Comparisons between the old and new equipment and utensils used at Highclere — very useful information

Many things have changed from the days of the old chamber pots, slipper baths and crock hot water bottles. When I first started work, soft soap out of a tin was used for washing floors and was put into the warm water. You washed floors on your hands and knees. Nowadays floors can be washed with a mop or an electric machine which can also dry them. Hard soap like Lifebuoy or Fairy was used to wash clothes or handwash whereas now non-biological powder/tablets are used for washing clothes. Liquid hand soap and creams are used for hands. Many new laws have been introduced because of the public. Non-slip liquid polish is essential and dries to a shine. It's labour saving, efficient and is sometimes dual purpose. Toilet paper – who will ever forget Izal? – was used in square packets. Today it's soft Andrex or something similar.

To clean windows, warm water, vinegar and newspaper were used. Nowadays there are so many products available but the most impressive that I've seen is something called Rainracer. It's a coating put on the windows by hand, with a light hosing of water washing off the dirt where necessary. The outside windows lasted for months, even the rain dribbled off the glass. It was used on ocean liners.

The Old: Solid fuel cookers. Coal, later anthracite, was used. Every couple of hours you had to fill the centre of the stove with fuel, the ashes were emptied every day and the flues cleaned out monthly. The heat was uncontrollable.
The New: Microwaves, turbo ovens, transportable calor gas ovens. These were

easier to use, transportable for outside catering, had faster cooking times and were more economical. Also, the temperature could be controlled.

The Old: Wooden sinks – for preparing vegetables, washing clothes, plucking and cleaning game. Grime and dirt collected and these sinks were very unhygienic.

The New: Stainless steel sinks. These complied with health and hygiene regulations and were easier to clean. There is more scope for outside catering as some are transportable. Game has to be specially prepared these days (unless for private use) to satisfy EEC rules.

The Old: Stone floors and duck boards – very cold, often cracked and also hard to clean. Wooden boards to stand on like a trellis to keep the feet from getting wet and cold from draughts.

The New: Non slip covering. Easier to clean. More hygienic. Easier on the legs and feet.

The Old: Wooden sieves. Pestle & Mortars. Bowls. Sieves as large as 12" in diameter with a wood tool that looked like a large mushroom to enable food to be pushed through the sieve. Large or small pestle & mortars were used, depending on herbs; also used for breaking up toffee and nuts. The bowls were for cakes, soufflés, sauces and whisking over hot water. Very time consuming, arm aching, sometimes inefficient.

The New: Liquidizers and food processors. Very versatile, quick and easy to use for the modern world we live in. Many years later the kitchen at Highclere Castle bought a Kenwood Mixer and Liquidizer. More thorough, capable of handling large amounts and much quicker. Convenient and labour saving.

The Old: Ice cream making. Ice cream was made by hand. Consisting of fresh fruit, double cream, egg whites and sometimes lemon juice, it was turned by hand using ice and rock salt in a wooden barrel, thus freezing the contents in the container.

The New: Ice cream making. Standard of ice cream is very high. Although homemade ice cream is still produced, the ice cream maker itself is driven by electricity, not turned by hand.

Statistics

During my time at Highclere I was often asked if I knew how many light bulbs there were. The answer? 482 excluding the fluorescents.

- It took 1 hour 52 minutes to lay the table for six people, complete with all the silver, in the State Dining Room. This included the time to remove the silver from the safe. During public opening the table was set for six, the seating was measured and also the place settings.

- It took 27 minutes to open the shutters on both floors.

- When preparing the Castle for opening, we needed 192 hours over a six-week period to polish the woodwork in the saloon, using fourteen 500g tins of polish and a lot of tender loving care. It hadn't been polished for nearly 70 years.

- It took 1 hour 32 minutes to dust the State Rooms and 35 minutes to dust the bedrooms.

- 58 minutes to buff the floors in the State Rooms.

- 33 minutes to dust mop the State Rooms.

- 65 minutes to hoover the State Rooms, 2 staircases, front hall and corridors and upstairs bedrooms.

- 4 hours 10 minutes to black lead the saloon fireplace.

- There are 4 main stairwells.

- There are 12 fireplaces in the main bedrooms and two in the offices.

- There are 7 fireplaces in the main State Rooms and one in the study.

- There were 365 pieces of crystal in the drawing room chandelier, but the total is 356 now.

- It took approximately 2 days to clean and polish the crystal chandelier.

- There are 386 windows, large and small, on two floors.

- It took 2 hours 23 minutes to polish the wooden shutters (both sides) in the boudoir.

- 37 minutes to wash the rear passage near the tea rooms.

- 21 minutes to polish the passage.

- 32 minutes to buff the polish off the floors and re-buff.